STRAW FOR FUEL, FEED AND FERTILISER?

By the same author

Cereal Straw (Oxford University Press)
Straw and Straw Craftsmen (Shire Publications)

STRAW FOR FUEL, FEED AND FERTILISER?

BY

A. R. STANIFORTH

FARMING PRESS LIMITED
WHARFEDALE ROAD, IPSWICH, SUFFOLK.

First published 1982
ISBN 0 85236 122 X

Set in eleven point Times and printed in Great Britain by Garden City Press Limited.

Contents

ILLUSTRATIONS

PLATES

FIGURES

FOREWORD
by
OLIVER WALSTON

THE discussion of straw burning generates almost as much heat as the act itself. As a result of these passions the actual problem has become obscured behind clouds of prejudice while farmers, conservationists, local Councils and members of the general public shout ever louder and more incoherently.

Arthur Staniforth has done the farming community a service by writing this book which is calm, objective and factual. He does not enter into the controversy by taking sides. Instead he has used the experience of a lifetime to look at the possible uses to which straw could be put. In a manner which is both clear and extremely practical, he describes the way straw has been used in different parts of the world as feed, fuel and fibre. Unlike so many commentators today, he does not minimise the problems but instead stresses that in today's economic climate burning is still the only realistic solution. However, in the future pressure from society may alter this and farmers must be prepared to change their attitudes.

This book will serve a vital purpose if it pursuades both farmers and the rest of society that straw need not necessarily be burnt and can be used for other purposes. The options are here for all of us to read. All that is now required is some commonsense and the will to think afresh.

OLIVER WALSTON
Thriplow Farm
Thriplow
Cambridgeshire

ACKNOWLEDGEMENTS

I am grateful to the Ministry of Agriculture, Fisheries and Food for the use of the results of surveys and trials carried out in various parts of England and Wales. I have also made free use of information contained in reports of the series of straw conferences organised by the Agricultural Development and Advisory Service in recent years at Oxford. Many colleagues and friends in the agricultural and ancillary industries have helped to gather the material. I would like in particular to thank Mr C.I. Harris, Mr P.L. Redman and Mr G.P. Shipway for looking through and discussing certain chapters. However, any errors and omissions as well as the general treatment of the subject are the responsibilty of the author alone. My appreciation goes to the photographers of the Ministry and to their Chief, the late Mr Tom Duffy, for their help over a number of years. Many of their pictures are included and thanks are due to Her Majesty's Stationery Office for permission to use these Crown copyright photographs. Other sources of illustrations are acknowledged with the captions.

Chapter 1

INTRODUCTION

THE USE AND DISPOSAL of a huge and growing surplus of straw presents British agriculture with one of its most serious problems. It is worth looking at the reasons for the emergence of this problem, if only to consider if any of the interlocking factors which have brought it about will change or can be changed.

VOLUME OF STRAW PRODUCTION

The first factor is the very great increase in the amount of cereals that are grown. It is not only that the area has increased; yields have approximately doubled in the past thirty years. Figure 1 shows production of wheat, barley and oats in England and Wales over the period 1955-81.

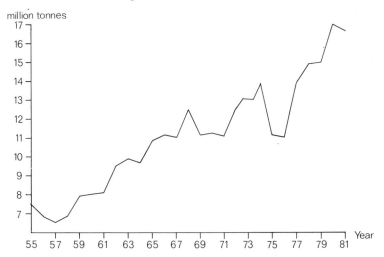

Fig. 1. Production of wheat, barley and oats in England and Wales, 1955-1981

Although the production of grain is known with some exactness, the production of straw from the cereal crop has not been so accurately measured. In the first place it is often not clear what is meant by 'straw production'.

If we take straw production to mean all the above-ground yield of the crop except the grain, and include all broken leaf, chaff and stubble, then it probably amounts to at least as much as the grain yield for most varieties. It is more usual to take as straw yield only the amount that is baled at an average stubble height and with a normally clean and tidy baling operation. Actual yields of baled straw have been measured in an Oxfordshire survey since 1974 by weighing sample bales in fields where the total area and number of bales produced have been recorded by the farmer. The annual average yields obtained from some six to ten fields of each crop and calculated at a standard 15 per cent dry matter are shown in figure 2.

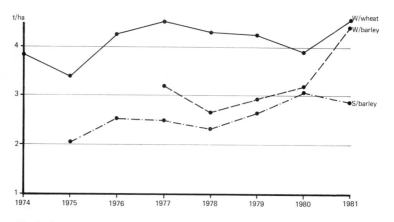

Fig. 2. Average annual straw yields for wheat, winter barley and oats, 1974-81, corrected to 15 per cent dry matter, obtained in Oxfordshire surveys.

This figure illustrates the type of fluctuations that might be expected from a small survey on randomly chosen farms, but there is a clear indication of a rising trend in the baled straw yields.

A much larger survey of straw yields on some 430 farms was carried out by ADAS in 1977 using a stratified sample of farms from the main cereal-growing areas. In the survey farmers were asked simply to estimate the number of bales and the weight of the bales removed from fields. From the data obtained the estimates of average straw yields shown in table 1 were calculated.

Table 1. Yield of baled straw, England and Wales, 1977

Crop	Tonnes per hectare
Wheat	4.0
Barley	3.1
Oats	3.8

These yields are not widely different from those obtained in the Oxfordshire survey in 1977.

There has been no national survey of baled straw yields since 1977, but it seems likely that these yields have been increasing with grain yields, though perhaps rather more slowly, during the past five years, particularly as the proportion of winter barley relative to spring barley has gone up. Baled straw yields are at present expected to average 4.2 tonnes per hectare for wheat, 3.3 tonnes per hectare for barley (winter and spring) and 4.0 tonnes per hectare for oats.

Basing the calculation on yields rising annually from the 1977 survey yields by 0.05 t/ha and the official estimated production area for the three main cereals for the five years 1977 to 1981, production may be estimated as in table 2.

Information about the quantities of straw that are actually baled each year is provided by Ministry of Agriculture surveys carried out in the autumn. These surveys are carried out on a stratified sample of some 2,500 cereal-growing farms in which the farmer is simply asked to give his estimate of the tonnage of straw which he baled in the past season. Table 3 shows the estimated total of straw production, the estimated total tonnage of straw baled and the 'surplus' straw production for the past five years.

Table 2. Straw production for wheat, barley and oats, England and Wales, 1977-81.

Year	Crop	Area '000 ha	Straw yield '000 tonnes	Total cereal straw yield '000 tonnes
1977	Wheat	1049	4196	—
	Barley	1882	5834	—
	Oats	127	483	10,513
1978	Wheat	1230	4982	—
	Barley	1808	5695	—
	Oats	120	462	11,139
1979	Wheat	1340	5494	—
	Barley	1796	5747	—
	Oats	86	335	11,576
1980	Wheat	1413	5864	—
	W. barley	721 ⎫	5944	—
	S. barley	1108 ⎭		
	Oats	105	415	12,223
1981	Wheat	1458	6124	—
	W. barley	790 ⎫	6046	—
	S. barley	1042 ⎭		
	Oats	100	400	12,570

Table 3. Straw yield, straw baled and surplus straw in England and Wales, 1977-81.

Year	Total straw production '000 tonnes	Straw baled '000 tonnes	Surplus straw '000 tonnes
1977	10,513	5370	5143
1978	11,139	4900	6239
1979	11,576	5365	6211
1980	12,223	5368	6855
1981	12,570	5107	7463

It can be seen that the amount of straw baled has remained fairly constant over this period at around 5 million tonnes while production has increased from about 10½ million to about 12½ million tonnes. The surplus of straw, most of which is now burned, is probably between 5 and 7 million tonnes. If, as is being predicted, the production of cereals increases in the next decade to over 20 million tonnes, straw production may well increase to 15 million tonnes and the surplus to 10 million tonnes per annum. The disposal of surplus straw presents a serious problem now, but the problem threatens to become worse. In parenthesis, mention should be made of the oilseed rape crop which has expanded during recent years to occupy more than 100,000 hectares and which has added to the problem of straw disposal.

It may be useful for some purposes to have a clear view of the geographical distribution of straw production in England and Wales. The National College of Agricultural Engineering at Silsoe has devised a means of showing the density of cereal straw production on a grid system, with the help of a computer. The map shown as figure 3 has been constructed by the NCAE in this way, using MAFF June census figures for parish cereal areas as basic data.

While straw production has been increasing steeply over the past quarter of a century, the combine harvester has taken over the harvesting of virtually all our cereal crops. Harvesting in the days of the binder was whole-crop harvesting and the straw was stacked after threshing for later use (Plate 1). With the advent of the combine the straw was simply dropped on the ground (Plate 2) and had to be dealt with in another series of operations. We have never solved the problem of dealing with the increasing surplus of straw left behind the combine—except by field burning. Balers and bale-handling systems may be improved in the future but, in the end, it is just possible that the best solution may lie in a return to a form of whole-crop harvesting and this will be discussed in Chapter 2.

Another factor in the growth of huge surpluses has been the growing specialisation of farming. This can be illustrated by considering the changes in cereal area and cattle population in three counties in eastern England. (Similar changes could be shown for other areas in the east of the country but recent alterations in county boundaries obscure the trends.)

For every head of cattle in 1955 there were 2.3 ha of cereals; but this had risen to 4 ha of cereals per head of cattle by 1980. The change in ratio is also a symptom of the decline in the

Fig. 3. Distribution of cereal straw production in England and Wales.

1.
Traditional English threshing scene—the straw was elevated from threshing machine to stack.

(Museum of English Rural Life)

2.
Great quantities of straw are today dropped behind the combine.

(Farmers Weekly)

Table 4. Total cereal area and total cattle numbers in Essex, Norfolk and Suffolk, 1955 and 1980

Cereals (ha)		Total Cattle	
1955	1980	1955	1980
1,059,775	1,379,663	452,747	345,155

importance of farmyard manure relative to 'artificial' fertiliser, particularly nitrogen, during this period.

ALTERNATIVES TO BURNING

The straw that is burned or wasted on British farms, if valued at £25 per tonne, would be approximately equal in value to that of the sugar beet crop at the farm gate. Yet there has been an insignificant effort put into the development of ways to utilise this huge resource. There has been a growing outcry from the public against a practice which seems to increase in scale, and this book takes a careful look at the advantages which can be claimed for field burning and at the possible alternatives that are open to the farmer.

The practical alternatives to field burning that are now available to the farmer come under three main headings. He could perhaps use some of it as fuel to replace purchased oil or coal or electricity. He may be able to use more straw as food for livestock—mainly for cattle and sheep. Or he can incorporate more straw in the soil, either after chopping it on the field or possibly after using it as litter for stock, including poultry. The incorporation of more chopped straw in the soil has to be seriously considered if only because this is the only way in which a large proportion of the great quantity that is at present burned could be otherwise dealt with in the immediate future.

There are some other possibilities for using straw away from the producing farm. These include the use of straw as fuel in horticulture or for domestic houses or for semi-industrial purposes such as drying hops or malt. There are also a number of industrial uses for the fibre in straw such as for paper and board-making. These industrial uses for straw off the farm will not be considered in detail here but farmers should bear in mind and do everything possible to encourage the development of markets for industrial uses which may lead to profitable sales of straw from the farm.

All straw users have to face the fact that it is a difficult material to deal with. It is all dropped on scattered fields within a few short weeks and is immediately at the mercy of our unpredictable weather. It is a very bulky material, hard to compress, awkward to transport and convey and requiring a great deal of room to store. Any plans for greater straw utilisation have to take into account these characteristics of the material. For this reason a section of the book is devoted to a survey of the methods of harvesting, collecting, processing, transporting and storing straw, with the emphasis on costs. It is essential to keep down the costs of handling straw if it is in the end to find economic uses.

Wherever possible the economic aspects of the various alternatives are considered. This inevitably means, in times of rapidly changing prices, that financial calculations become out of date. For this reason, the financial information is throughout supported by fundamental data, so that the reader can recalculate the sums using his own up-to-date costs and prices.

Whenever possible the 1982 edition of the Wye College *Farm Management Pocketbook*, edited by John Nix, has been used as a source of economic information. In some of the costings it is necessary to include an element which is due to capital expenditure on machinery or buildings. There are various ways of allocating such capital costs and tax consider-ations, not to speak of capital availability, may influence calculations. The method employed here is to add an annual write-off charge based on the standard amortisation tables from the Wye College Handbook; these tables are shown at Appendix 2.

Chapter 2

FROM HARVEST TO STORAGE

ANY CONSIDERATION of ways in which straw can be used must begin with calculations of costs of removing it. Under the traditional system of cutting with the binder, carting to stack yard and threshing when convenient, the orderly movement of the straw from cornfield to straw stack was tied in with the movement of the grain. The straw became available in the loose, long state at a central place on the farm for traditional uses such as feed and litter for livestock, thatching and, occasionally, for sale off the farm. The coming of the combine, coinciding as it did with greatly increased acreages and yields of cereal crops, found the British farmer unprepared to deal with the large quantity of straw remaining in the field. This chapter looks at various aspects of moving straw after combining, some of them interrelated.

A further section is devoted to whole-crop harvesting. It may be that the combine harvester, as at present designed, will prove in the end to be an unsatisfactory method of harvesting cereals in areas of the world which cannot afford to discard one half of the dry matter production of cereal crops. Combine harvesters will certainly not disappear overnight, but a few farmers are already experimenting with whole-crop harvesting systems and it is well worth looking carefully at what is involved in modern systems of gathering in both grain and straw.

One general point needs to be emphasised in any calculations that are made about harvesting and moving straw from the field—the great variability of the British climate. Figure 4 shows how, in one part of the country, seasons have varied over a period of thirty years during which very dry summers provided up to fifty dry days in the months of August and September, whereas in wetter seasons there have been as few as twenty dry days in these months. To make sure that straw is

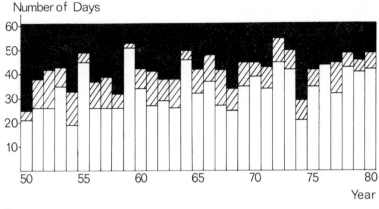

Key:

- ■ Wet Days
- ▨ Up to 1mm Rain
- ▢ Dry Days(less than 1mm Rain)

Fig. 4. Record of wet and dry days at Oxford, August and September, 1950-80.

harvested in a dry, undamaged condition it is essential to be able to collect and transport it to store immediately after combining. This means that the farmer will need sufficient manpower and machinery of his own to do the work or he must be able to rely upon a contractor to do it for him.

Before going on to describe various systems for moving, processing and storing straw it has to be said that there is a dearth of reliable information about the output and efficiency of some of them. Nevertheless it is hoped that the information in this chapter will assist in planning the economic utilisation of straw.

HARVESTING STRAW

Field Baling
The system of packaging straw at the back of the combine which

was developed for some of the early models proved impractical for most farmers. The bundles were too loosely packed and easily soaked by rain, and took too much time to collect and stack. Yet a few of these machines survived for many years on some potato-growing farms because the bundles were very convenient for covering potato clamps. It might seem surprising that combine manufacturers did not develop attachments which would make dense bales—but the additional weight and power requirement ruled this out. The pick-up baler originally developed for hay baling has been the standard machine for collecting straw.

For many years the 'conventional' baler, producing rectangular bales of about 15 to 20 kg which could be moved by hand, was normally used to bale straw. More recently the big 'square' and big 'round' balers have been introduced; they make bales which commonly weigh between 250 and 350 kg and have to be mechanically handled. During the past few seasons big 'square' balers which make bales about 50 per cent more dense than conventional balers have been brought into use. They have a high rate of work but are expensive to buy. Their use can be justified only when they can be used to bale large tonnages, which usually means that they are contractors' machines.

The following table summarises some of the main features of available types of balers. The figures shown are subject to considerable variation according to circumstances. Bale sizes,

Table 5. Indications of bale size, weights and densities of various baler types with estimated average baler costs and work rates

Baler type	Bale dimensions m	Bale weight kg	Bale density kg/m3	Output t/hour	Baler cost £
Conventional	0.36 × 0.46 × 0.99	18	80–140	5*	2500–4000
Big 'square'	1.5 × 1.5 × 2.33	300	55– 80	7	6000–7500
Big 'round'	1.4 (diam.) × 1.5	340	50– 80	7	6000–7500
Big 'square'	1.25 × 1.25 × 2.65	600	120–160	15	25,000-30,000
Stack wagon	2.4 × 6 × 2.7	2300	60	7–12†	—

* used with flat–8 accumulator
† output to field side

weights and densities vary according to the make of the baler, how it is adjusted and the condition of the straw. Rates of work can differ appreciably depending on the state of the straw, the way it is rowed up, the type of tractor used and other factors. Nevertheless table 5 gives an indication of features which have to be taken into account in comparing straw-baling systems. Although not in the strict sense a baling machine, stack wagon details are included in the table for comparison.

There is an almost endless variety of systems for accumulating, packaging, moving and transporting various types of bales. These have been described in various publications, including 'Balers and Bale Handling', Mechanisation Leaflet No 16 published by MAFF, 1977. These systems are continually being improved and no attempt will be made here to describe them. The most important point to bear in mind is that systems for baling *and* removal have to be designed to clear the field of straw and get it under cover as soon as possible after combining. It can be seen that the first three systems in table 5 can more or less keep up with a large combine cutting 1½ ha per hour yielding 6 tonnes of straw while the large-capacity, high-density, 'square' baler should be able to clear up behind at least two large combines.

Forage Harvesters

Straw may also be harvested from the swath by using forage harvesters chopping into trailers, as for silage. Flail, double-chop and precision-chop harvesters can be used. Precision-chop forage harvesters are generally more expensive and require more powerful tractors, but they are capable of chopping the straw into 5 cm lengths whereas the flail and double-chop harvesters give only a limited chop. All three methods are most suitable for short hauls because of the very low density of the loose straw. Work rates of 2 tonnes per hour of dry matter per man from field to store have been obtained.

Stack Wagons

American-style stack wagons (Plate 3) have been demonstrated in this country. They pick up straw from the swath with a flail-pick-up type harvester and blow it into high-sided trailers. The entire load can then be unloaded by belts in the base of the

3.
A 'stack wagon' discharging chopped straw in Oregon, USA.
(T.R. Miles)

trailer to form a 'stack'. Wagons with dimensions of approximately
2.4 × 6 × 2.7 m form stacks of about 2.3 tonnes and rates of
removal to field side of between about 6 and about 12 tonnes
per hour have been reported from thick crops. The chop length
for stack wagons working in straw is between 5 and 30 cm. The
density of these loads, at about 60 kg/m³, restricts economic
transport over long distances. Self-loading forage wagons are
also available but they have the disadvantage of a very low
density load. Prior to storage the load is chopped so that 70 per
cent is less than 5 cm long and it has been found that, at this
length of chop, the straw when stored in bulk will settle to a
density of between 100 and 130 kg/m³.

Field Cubing
Field cubing from the swath has been attempted using machines
that have been developed for lucerne. However, cube formation
has proved more difficult with straw and no machine is on the
market at the present time which will give sufficient output at an
acceptable power input for cereal straw. In the United States
trials of a field cuber of the ring and die type showed that it took
18.2 MJ of energy to cube one kilogram of straw—rather more
than the gross energy in the straw.

Whole-Crop Harvesting

It may come as a surprise to some that several thousand hectares of wheat are annually harvested by the traditional method, using the binder, in England south of a line from the Severn to the Wash. The reason for the survival of the practice on this scale is that it still pays some cereal growers—mainly those with relatively small areas of wheat—because there is a market for some 15,000 tonnes annually of the straw for thatching. The procedure is as follows:

The wheat crop should be of a variety yielding straw of at least 70 cm length and it must be a good standing crop. It is cut with a binder before it is fully 'combine ripe', preferably when the nodes or knees are still green and the heads erect. After cutting, the crop is normally stooked in the traditional manner and left in the field for a week or two—perhaps to hear church bells ring three times—so that the ears and straw can mature. It is then usually loaded on to trailers and stacked to await the threshing drum, though occasionally it is threshed straight from the stook. The stacks are sometimes in barns but are often made out of doors with a PVC sheet as covering. A specially adapted threshing drum which beats only the ears of the corn is used for reed production. These machines carry the straw forward horizontally between belts, comb out the loose leaves, weeds and short straws and then tie up the combed reed in bundles ready for the thatcher (Plate 4).

The price for wheat reed in recent years has fluctuated around £300 per tonne at the thatching site. The wheat crop is normally cut with a low stubble and total harvested straw yields of around 7 tonnes per hectare are obtainable. The yield of combed reed is often about half of the total straw yield. Experience on an Oxfordshire farm in 1980 gives an indication of the economic results which may be obtained from growing wheat for reed. Growing costs are roughly average for the crop but the harvesting and stacking of approximately 8 hectares took five men ten working days and a team of six people was required for threshing. This obviously increased costs considerably over normal combining costs. However, there were no drying or storage costs, apart from the depreciation on a stack sheet which costs £350 for 176 sq m and is likely to last for at least three years.

Table 6. Outputs and costs for wheat reed production on an Oxfordshire farm in 1980. Figures are per hectare.

Output	£
Grain: 6.2 tonnes at £105	649
Combed reed: 3.29 tonnes at £271	892
Bedding straw: 3.19 tonnes at £15	48
Chaff (none saved)	—
Total	1589

Costs	
Growing costs: seed: fertiliser etc.	198
Bindering, stoking, stacking, twine, threshing, paid labour	388
Total Costs	586
SURPLUS OR GROSS MARGIN	1003

4.
A form ·of whole-crop harvesting—wheat 'reed', baled combings and chaff are all saved along with the grain on an Oxfordshire farm in 1980.
(Crown copyright)

Particularly for the small producer who is prepared to go to the extra trouble and who wishes to intensify output from a limited area, the system has attractions. In addition to the extra income from the reed it is worth mentioning that the combings have a better analysis as a feed than normal straw and the chaff is being used by some producers in the traditional way for feeding horses.

Modern Whole-crop Harvesting

Two main systems have been under trial in recent years, one pioneered on a large scale in Sweden and the other at the Nottingham University School of Agriculture at Sutton Bonington. Both entail harvesting the whole crop by means of a type of forage harvester and bringing it in for processing.

The Swedish system depended upon large and complicated central separation and processing plants serving several thousand hectares of cereals. Self-propelled forage harvesters chopped the crop into 3-5 centimetre lengths and blew it into de-mountable containers with 40 m³ capacity. The chopped whole crop settled to a density approximately twice that of conventional bales so that the containers held about 8 tonnes of crop. Both the harvesters and the trailers had to be of rugged construction for possibly 24-hours-per-day work. Some idea of the logistics of the operation is given by the calculation that an output of 30 tonnes per hour would be needed over a period of fifty working days of twenty-four hours to clear a crop of 9 tonnes per ha from 4,000 ha. It can be calculated that between two and eight 8-tonne trailers travelling at 15 km per hour would be needed to move this crop to a separating plant over distances from 3 to 15 km, assuming no breakdowns or other delays.

The Sutton Bonington system is a more modest conception. Ordinary full-chop harvesters are used, blowing the crop into 20 m³ silage trailers of 4-tonne capacity. It has been found that cutting with quite a high stubble leads to less abrasion and knife wear than grass cutting and that once-a-day sharpening of the blades is sufficient. Grain is separated from straw by means of a J-type auger which tips the mixture over the edge of the conveyor in a continuous band through which an air stream is blown. The fact that separation is carried out on the undried material enables the subsequent drying of the grain fraction to be done more simply and efficiently. With the experience that has been built up on the use of straw as a fuel for grain drying there seems to be no reason why straw from the separator should not be efficiently used as a fuel, even though it is too moist for optimum energy output. Not all the straw will be required for fuel and a large bulk is likely to remain. On mixed farms it may be possible to treat this, either chemically or by drying, for storage and later feeding to livestock. On farms with few or no livestock, it would obviously be wise not to venture into whole-crop harvesting until profitable outlets of the surplus straw can be assured.

The Sutton Bonington system is being adapted for use on a private mixed farm in the Midlands. This farmer is whole-crop harvesting his barley crop with an adapted forage harvester and extra-high-sided trailers with 26 m³ capacity. He uses a winnower with a 10 tonne per hour throughput, blowing the straw direct to a barn for ammonia treatment for cattle feeding, and the grain into storage after treating with sodium hydroxide. In this way he avoids the need to dry the crop.

On this farm the crop is separated into two fractions only—grain and the remainder of straw and chaff—and the separation need not be absolutely complete because the object is to feed both fractions to cattle. This in turn permits a high rate of work by the separator. However, the system can be adapted to give several points of take-off in the separator according to the air resistance of the particles, and this more complete fractionation could be important for some industrial uses of straw.

It is still too early to say whether the Sutton Bonington system can be developed for wider practical application, but it shows promise of succeeding on this animal/livestock farm where it is being adopted in a step-by-step process over several seasons to meet special requirements. It is a flexible system and could be adapted to more specialised arable farms if the straw output could be used as fuel or sold for commercial use. Harvesting with full-chop harvesters has given 3 per cent to 4 per cent of broken grains and microscopic examination of the forage-harvested crop has not shown any greater damage to the grain than is made by ordinary combine harvesters.

The advantages of whole-crop harvesting are widely recognised. The harvester is less dependent than the combine harvester on really dry weather to work satisfactorily, and the straw is brought to a central point where it can be more conveniently used or processed. It is also quite easy to separate out the more nutritionally valuable chaff and lighter fractions of the straw from the more fibrous internodes which may be best suited to paper- or board-making.

The disadvantages of the system are mainly related to the bulk of the material that has to be harvested and separated within a comparatively short time.

Collecting Chaff from Combine Harvesters

A chaff-saving attachment to the combine harvester (Plate 5), developed in Saskatchewan, goes some of the way towards whole-crop harvesting. A 23 cm auger collects all the chaff, light grain, broken leaf and weed seed that comes over the sieves and a 50 cm fan blows the material into an enclosed trailer of 10 cubic metre capacity which holds up to 700 kg of the tailings. This miniature stack wagon can be unloaded on the move by a pull rope and the material can be collected later by fore-end loader—it is said to become more compact if allowed to settle for a few days.

5.
A chaff-saving attachment made in Saskatchewan.

The system helps to prevent volunteer growth of grain and to reduce the spread of weed seeds, as well as providing a supply of forage. No laboratory analyses of the saved tailings are available, but some Canadian cattle feeders use combine-harvested oat tailings as a substitute for medium-quality hay. The material is sometimes fed with silage in troughs. Wheat chaff could also provide useful feed, but barley tailings are considered inferior in Canada.

The auger, chaff blower and wagon cost about $3,000 Canadian in North America. The attachment can be made to fit any size of combine and is V-belt-driven from a pulley on the combine. The power requirement is low and is said not to interfere with combine operation.

TRANSPORT

For road transport over any considerable distance it is difficult, if not impossible, to carry a full pay-load with normal straw bales as is shown in table 7.

A 12 m flat-bed trailer, for a full pay-load of 24 tonnes in a volume of 90 cubic metres would need a minimum bulk density

Table 7. Straw-carrying capacity of 12 tonne lorry (7.5m bed length, 12t maximum payload)

Bale type	Dimensions (m)	Load formation	Bales per load	Total load weight (t)
Big square	1.5 × 1.5 × 2.33	2 layers × 5 on bed 1 bale above cab	11	3.6
Big round (reduced diameter* from 1.8m)	1.4 diam. × 1.5	5 groups of 1 above 2 on bed 1 bale above cab	16	4.3
Big round (narrow)	1.4 diam. × 1.2	2 layers × 10 on bed, 2 bales above cab	22	6.0
Conventional	0.36 × 0.46 × 0.99	8 layers × 40 on bed, 30 bales above cab	350	6.3

* Diameter reduced and cylindrical axes set longitudinally on lorry bed to keep load width within legal requirements.

6.
An uneconomic load of big round bales.

(Crown copyright)

of 260 kg per cubic metre. It is clear that bale densities of 100 kg per cubic metre are much too low to give full pay loads (Plate 6).

Legal Limits to Load Dimensions

When considering road transport it is necessary to remember the *legal limits to load dimensions.* United Kingdom regulations state that loads of bales must not project more than 305 mm on either side of the vehicle or trailer and that the overall width of the load must not exceed 2.9 m. For the most economical transport, bale dimensions should be such that they allow the load to be placed so that the legal width is closely approached but not exceeded.

PROCESSING

Densification of Bales

Bales can be compressed in hydraulic presses, and work at the Cranfield Institute of Technology showed that a standard straw bale could be compressed down to about one-third of its length under comparatively low pressure. However, the pressure and therefore the energy needed to reduce the bale down to about one-tenth of the original length rose very steeply. This is illustrated in figure 5.

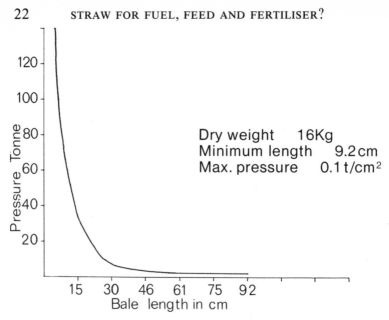

Fig. 5. Compression of straw bale 46 × 36 × 92cm.

Prototype presses have now been made which will reduce standard and big bales to approximately one-third of their original volume and to a density of around 300 kg per cubic metre (Plate 7). Such densified bales can be satisfactorily retied with heavy twine, but the development of automatic tying and knotting has yet to be completed. When fully developed, these bale compressors are expected to work at an output of up to 4 tonnes per hour, but it is not yet possible to put a firm figure on the cost of the process. It seems, however, unlikely to be less than £5.00 per tonne. The economic advantage in improved efficiency of storage and transport could more than pay for the cost of such bale densification. The denser bale has already been shown to enable sufficient straw fuel to be stoked into certain straw-burning boilers to last through the night, whereas conventional bales burn out after a few hours.

Cubing or Pelleting Straw after Field Harvesting

This involves double-handling of the crop, but it enables the field to be quickly cleared by baling and carting, and is the only

7.
Prototype bale-compressing machine built by Messrs Abbott and Trower, Alton, Hants.

(Crown copyright)

practical method of cubing straw at present. Using standard presses, straw can be cubed to densities up to 650 kg per cubic metre or even higher with suitable binders, but the power requirement has so far proved to be high. There has been considerable research into more economical methods of pelleting or briquetting waste organic matter. A standard piston-type extrusion press has been shown at the NIAE to have a high power requirement and low output; roller extrusion presses tend to have a good output, but a heavy power demand. The screw extrusion type of pelleter has given promising results with citrus pulp, but may be unsuitable for straw; the gear cuber designed in Oregon gave promising results, but suffered severely from wear, as do most presses working with straw.

The fact that the straw has to be chopped or ground before it can be put through the press adds to the power requirement and cost of the process. It has been shown to be essential for efficient chopping and pressing that the straw has a moisture content no higher than about 16 per cent; this means that only straw which is baled when really dry and carefully stored will be suitable. To have to add the cost of drying straw may render the process of compaction uneconomic.

Chopping and Grinding

There is renewed interest in methods of reducing straw to relatively small particles for use as fuel, feed, livestock bedding, industrial purposes and for return to the land.

A great variety of methods and machines are available for chopping and grinding straw, and the following systems are briefly described simply in order to illustrate the range of possibilities. It is notoriously difficult to give precise output/power relationships for straw choppers—so much depends upon straw quality, in particular its moisture content. High moisture contents usually reduce output severely.

1. Forage harvesters

Robust models of forage harvesters (Plate 8) are necessary to

8.
A forage harvester used to chop straw; hand feeding is needed.

(Author)

cope with continuous work on straw. The best full-chop harvesters can give a 5 cm chop with a power requirement in excess of 50 hp and an output of up to 4 tonnes per hour when used as stationary units, but they normally have to be fed by hand.

2. Traditional chaff cutters

The chop can be adjusted from about 0.5 cm to about 7 cm. Very cheap hand-driven models are still available but they are also obtainable with small (1-1½ hp) electric motors and they can be fitted with automatic mechanical or pneumatic discharge. They can give an output of 350-450 kg per hour, increasing as length of cut increases; but, again, must be fed by hand.

3. Hammer mills

There are a number of hammer mills available which can handle straw. Most have to be fed manually but in some cases this can be automated. Some can take whole bales. They can be fitted with screens of various sizes to suit the length of chop required, or they can be used with the screen removed. Outputs vary with screen size, power input and quality of straw but hammer mills in general have a high power requirement per tonne output of straw milled. A few models can blow the milled straw for a distance up to about 20 m and ducting is also available on at least one model. One effect of hammer milling to a very small particle size may be of practical importance in some circumstances. When hammer-milled through a 3 mm screen the density of straw is greatly increased to around 180 kg/m^3.

4. Tub grinders

Hammers rotating through stationary teeth in the bottom of the tub create a scissor action. The larger tub grinders (Plate 9) will take any size of bale and, as they rotate, they bring the bales into contact with the grinder. Screen sizes of between approximately 0.5 cm and 10 cm are available. Outputs of straw from the larger machines which require at least 100 hp to drive them may be about 4 tonnes per hour at a particle length of about 2 cm or up to 8 tonnes per hour at particle length of about 7 cm. The product is partially shredded as well as chopped. Tub grinders

9.
A large tub grinder can accept any size of bale; this one is being hand-fed with conventional bales.

(Crown copyright)

have the advantage of being mobile and well suited to operation by contractors. The cost of tub grinding will depend upon many factors. Assuming a tractor costing £14,000 and a tub grinder costing £7,000, with the tractor working 1,000 hours and the tub grinder working 200 hours per annum, there would be a machinery cost per hour of about £12, including depreciation, tax and insurance, repairs and maintenance and fuel and oil, but not including labour. Assuming an output of 4 tonnes per hour, the cost of grinding works out at a little less than £4 per tonne. If the machines are used for fewer hours or if damp straw is used, giving a lower throughput, then costs will rise. Contractors usually charge by the hour and, with dry straw and a good rate of work, contract tub grinding may cost about £10 per tonne or somewhat less.

A small type of tub grinder (Plate 10) has recently been marketed which takes conventional bales and is powered by a 7.5 hp petrol engine. It can be hand-pushed to be used in, for instance, poultry houses or cow kennels. In this machine knives rotate through stationary bars (Plate 11) at the bottom of the tub and the length of chop is adjustable. At an average chop length

10.
A small Canadian-made tub grinder which takes conventional bales and can be hand-pushed.

(Crown copyright)

of about 3 cm an output of approximately 500 kg per hour can be expected with dry straw. The bales have to be placed in the tub by hand.

5. Bale shredders and choppers
There is now available a great variety of machinery specifically designed to shred conventional bales, often using a flail cutter type of action. Many of these machines are pto-driven and some are tractor linkage-mounted.

6. Disc refiners
Another method of grinding straw is to put it through a disc refiner in which one rotating disc with suitable plate con-figuration rotates on another stationary disc. These machines are used in the production of pulp for the paper industry. The disc refiner has the effect of exposing the fine fibres in straw to enzyme action. This very severe grinding of straw could

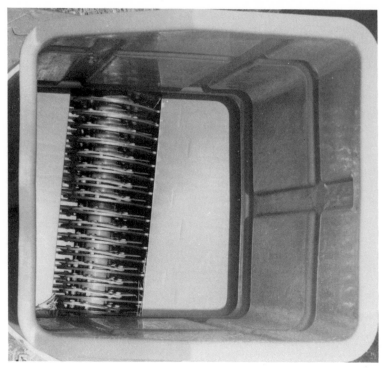

11.
Looking into small tub grinder, showing how rotating knives operate between fixed bars.

(Crown copyright)

theoretically improve its digestibility but the cost is prohibitively high. A machine tested in the United States treated about 220 kg per hour, using an average of 55 kW.

Conveying

When cereals were harvested by binder and threshed in a traditional way the movement of straw and chaff was well understood. The loose straw was conveyed on the elevator or pitcher the required distance to the straw stack. The pitcher consisted of long, backward-pointing spikes mounted on an endless chain which dragged the straw as it dropped from the straw walkers up a smooth channel until it fell off at the feet of a man with a pitchfork who moved it on. These elevators rarely

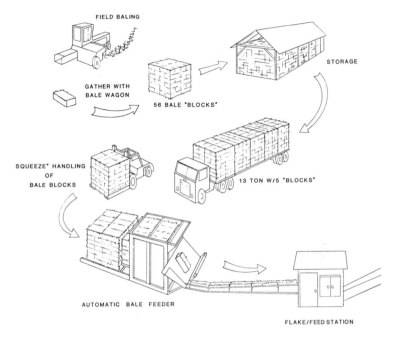

Fig. 6. An American system of moving conventional bales from field to processor.

(T.R. Miles)

gave trouble except in windy weather. The chaff was generally saved and it was occasionally possible to blow it in ducting directly into the chaff house; otherwise it was bagged off and a man would tip it in the chaff house.

Many methods of conveying straw are now under trial. One system, based on the 'conventional' rectangular bale, is illustrated in figure 6. Conveniently sized packs are moved from field to store and from store to the site at which they are to be used. There the packs are placed into an automatic bale feeder which reverses the process of the field accumulator and feeds single bales into the bale track conveyor. They can then be fed into choppers or shredders for combustion or further processing. High-density big rectangular bales would not lend themselves to this system but they can be efficiently dealt with as units weighing approximately 600 kg by the larger tub grinders.

When straw is required for some form of processing it is

often necessary to chop or shred it. Augers have been successfully used in some factories to move the chopped straw but trouble can be experienced on long runs at auger-bearing points. The low density of chopped straw can result in bridging in the hoppers from which it is gravity fed to the auger, and special censors have been devised to detect such bridging.

Pneumatic conveying of chopped straw is reported to give excellent results and great reliability over considerable distances in some Eastern European pulp mills using straw. It is also used with success in some small processing plants in France. No information is available as to power requirement but this is often high with pneumatic systems.

For horizontal or near horizontal conveying, belt conveyors give good results. When space is restricted they can be used as an alternative to a forage box in moving, for instance, chopped straw to milking goats.

Dust
Any discussion of straw chopping and conveying would be incomplete without mention of the dust problem which is encountered with most systems. The level of dust may be reduced by the use of closed systems and extractors, but farm staff using chopping and conveying equipment should always wear the correct type of dust mask.

When straw choppers and grinders are used in open situations and in breezy or windy weather, and particularly if any form of elevator is used, there is a great tendency for the material to be blown away into gutters and troughs and this can cause a considerable nuisance. Whenever possible it is best to carry out this work in still weather and often it is well worth while erecting a reliable windbreak.

STORAGE

When it is to be used in the long state for bedding livestock, the moisture content of straw is not a critical matter. This is particularly true in the case of littering uncovered yards. However, if it is to be used for feeding or if it is to be chopped or processed in any way, or used for fuel, it is important that straw

12.
A stack of conventional bales with ventilation tunnels.

(Crown copyright)

13.
Same type of stack as plate 12 at the end of winter with about 30 per cent of straw spoiled.

(Crown copyright)

should be kept dry. Figure 7 (page 44) shows how moisture content reduces the fuel value of straw. When it comes to milling or chopping straw, it has been shown that machine output can be greatly increased by reducing straw moisture content from 20 per cent to 12 per cent. Moisture content has also been shown to be crucial when straw is to be cubed or briquetted—satisfactory cubing may be impossible at moisture contents above 17 per cent. Microbiological activity in straw increases rapidly as moisture content rises; harmful moulds, for instance, may increase and render the straw toxic.

Satisfactory, economic methods of straw storage are therefore essential in plans for the increased use of straw. The following paragraphs consider the technical and economic efficiency of various methods that have been tried.

Methods without Cover
Conventional bales are sometimes seen in stacks which have been carefully constructed with pitched roofs. These will shed a certain amount of rainfall and may be reasonably satisfactory for a few months after harvest. Conventional bales have commonly been stored in flat-roofed stacks in which ventilation tunnels have been left in the last layer but one (Plate 12). These tunnels are designed to allow free air circulation so that bales that are rained on can dry out. This may be effective for light showers but invariably these stacks begin to deteriorate after Christmas, and as much as 30 per cent of the straw is often spoiled by the end of the winter (Plate 13).

Big round bales left in the open will also shed light showers and will dry out quickly in good weather. Some big round balers are designed to pack the outer layers more tightly so as to deflect more precipitation. However, even the best-made big round bales inevitably absorb moisture as the season progresses and they will tend to dry out only slowly in spells of prolonged damp weather.

It has been claimed that chopped straw can be stored in uncovered heaps and this may be true for a limited period of weather which is not too wet. However these heaps eventually allow rain to seep in and cause damage, and this method cannot be recommended for any but very short-term storage.

None of the methods of storing straw out of doors without

cover can be considered satisfactory and reliable for more than a very short period in the British climate if the straw is to be used for anything but bedding.

Methods with Cover but no Buildings

Polythene sheeting has been used, either over the top of the stack or placed beneath the top layer of bales. It is a cheap method but has proved unreliable. Thin-gauge sheeting is almost useless but even 1000-gauge sheet becomes perished or punctured, and rainwater soon penetrates the holes and ruins the straw beneath. In a series of careful trials in East Anglia a good-quality plastic sheet was placed over narrow stacks of big rectangular bales and carefully netted down to minimise flapping (Plate 14). These stacks were regularly inspected and holes or tears that developed were taped up. Eventually the system was abandoned as unsatisfactory.

Butyl rubber sheeting has also been tried but it is heavy to handle, comparatively expensive and proved liable to damage by vermin; it cannot be advised.

PVC sheeting, reinforced with nylon, has proved a more satisfactory covering material. It can be purchased eyeletted and roped in suitable sizes for about £2.40 per sq metre at the time of writing. It has been claimed to last five years but it might be safer to budget on a three year life and even for this it is important that rodents should not attack it. This sheeting is in regular use to cover corn stacks destined for threshing for thatching straw, and it is generally passing this test satisfactorily.

Another covering which has given good results over a number of years in Hampshire has been galvanised iron sheets (Plate 15). These sheets can often be purchased cheaply as reject sheets, or secondhand, at a cost of around £4.00 per sq metre. The bale stacks should be made so that there is a very slight pitch to one side; the sheets are laid on with a small overlap and covered with a final layer of bales. A disadvantage compared with PVC sheeting is that there is no overhang (to avoid lifting by wind) and this means that the shed water will tend to run down the outside of the stack; but in practice the damage is usually slight. However, the top layer of bales is unprotected and will be spoilt. There is also a considerable labour demand in putting on, taking off, transporting and storing the sheets themselves.

14.
Big square bales covered with netted polythene in stacklets. The
system was only partially successful.

(Author)

15.
A large stack with roof of corrugated galvanised sheets held down by
one layer of bales. The system has been successful over several years
but the sides of the stack are unprotected.

(Crown copyright)

16.
Storage in large barns—an excellent system but costly.

(Author)

Storage in Buildings

Storage in buildings is undoubtedly the most reliable method of keeping straw dry. Large, high barns (Plate 16) are the best for mechanised handling and it is an advantage if the weather side is enclosed. Some farmers find that they have considerable covered storage available in redundant livestock buildings, but new buildings will often be needed if there is to be a large increase in the tonnage of stored straw. Sometimes the barns can be put to another use when not holding straw, but this will be unlikely when the straw has to be kept over the winter.

Storage Costs

The following table compares the cost of storing straw by different methods. The costs given are averages at the time of writing and there is room for adjustment in the expected life of materials in the light of experience. All calculations assume a stack height of 5 metres and are based on a standard bale density of 100 kg per m³. The cost of storage per tonne is made up of an annual share of the cost over the estimated life plus an annual interest charge of 15 per cent on total capital outlay as shown in brackets.

Table 8. Theoretical costs of storing straw

Type of storage	Cost/m² £	Life in years	Cost of storage per tonne £
PVC sheet	2.40	3	2.32 (1.60 plus 0.72)
Galvanised sheets	4.00	5	2.80 (1.60 plus 1.20)
Pole barn	7.00	10	3.50 (1.40 plus 2.10)
Steel or concrete barn	16.00	20	6.40 (1.60 plus 4.80)

The economics of straw storage are greatly affected by the shape and density of bales. Square bales with a density of 150 kg/m³ will cost one-third less than square bales with a density of 100 kg/m³, while big round bales, which take up more space in store, will cost perhaps one-third more. One of the cheapest ways of storing straw at the present time is in big square bales with a density of 150 kg/m³ under PVC sheeting—such storage is possible at around £1.50 per tonne.

When Dutch barns are put up mainly for the purpose of storing straw it will pay to make them high. Some farmers have erected storage barns measuring 8 m to the eaves, costing little more per square metre covered than barns 5 m high at the eaves. By so doing and by having very dense bales the cost of barn storage can be reduced by about £1 per tonne below that shown in Table 8.

Moisture Content of Straw

Moisture content is often critical to the efficient processing or combustion of straw and the matter frequently comes up in discussion.

The moisture content of straw left behind the combine in eastern England will usually be between 8 per cent in very hot, dry weather and 20 per cent in cool, moist conditions. Assuming that there is no precipitation, straw lying loose in the open air will reach an equilibrium moisture content which depends on the relative humidity of the atmosphere. The relationship between moisture content and relative humidity follows the pattern shown in Table 9.

**Table 9. Equilibrium values for the moisture content
of straw at different relative humidities**

Relative humidity of air %	Straw moisture content %
95	35
90	30
80	21.5
77	20
70	16
60	12.5

In fact, the relationship is no so simple as shown in that table because, for a given relative humidity, the moisture content of the straw will increase slightly as temperature drops and decrease as temperature rises.

Straw moisture content does not change instantaneously with a change in relative humidity. When the straw is loose and air can move freely around it, it may reach a new equilibrium in a matter of hours. But when it is packed tightly in bales, and particularly if stacked in large bulk, the process of taking up or releasing moisture will be much slower. After the damp 1974 harvest straw was being taken from covered store in mid-winter at a moisture content of more than 20 per cent; this straw was caked and affected by mould, and some mould is likely to develop in straw which is tightly baled and cannot be aired at moisture contents above 16 per cent.

It is obviously important to bale straw when its moisture content is below 16 per cent. In good combining weather this may often best be done by baling immediately after the combine, particularly if there is any risk of rain.

If dry straw with a moisture content of between, say, 10 and 15 per cent is put immediately into a covered store which is protected on the windward side, it will take up moisture only slowly, even when the relative humidity is high. Equally, of course, damp straw stored under similar conditions will not dry out quickly.

Several types of moisture meter are now available for testing straw bales. They can sometimes give rather erratic readings if there is green matter in bales or if bales are unevenly packed since they depend upon electrical conductivity for their readings. However, they are a useful aid in determining the moisture content of stored straw (Plate 17).

Precautions to Take when Storing Straw

Rats and mice can be a serious nuisance in stored straw— particularly when they eat through the bale bands. Poison baiting will usually control these rodents if it is properly carried out. Drainpipes conveniently placed among the bales will facilitate baiting, but it is better to put the bait down in good time at a distance from the stored straw, on the route followed by the rats as they come in from the fields after harvest. In this way most of them will be killed before they enter the storage area. It is more difficult to poison mice than rats but some new poisons are now available that are effective even if the mice are resistant to Warfarin. A few good cats around the yards can help to control mice and young rats. Rodent control is dealt with in more detail in ADAS leaflets 608 and 627.

17.
Testing bale moisture content.

(Crown copyright)

The siting of stacks is important. As with corn stacks, it is essential to choose a dry base and to insulate from rising damp. It is also wise not to place stacks close together in case of fire and, if there is to be a line of stacks, put the line at right-angles to the direction of the prevailing wind.

It is important to insure stacks against fire—particularly so when straw is contracted for or when it has to supply a definite need which would require it to be replaced without delay. On most farms straw is included in a general fire risk policy and may cost about £0.50 per tonne, but it may be prudent to insure it as a separate item if, for instance, an enterprise is dependent on it for fuel. In such cases it should be insured at a value equivalent to full replacement cost.

Chapter 3

STRAW FOR FUEL

GLIDER PILOTS like to steer into the convection currents above straw fires that lift the gliders swiftly to great heights. In this way a tiny fraction of the store of energy in field-burned straw is put to some small purpose. How much energy is there in this straw? How does it compare with the total amount of energy that the agricultural industry uses? And what prospects are there of using more of the energy that now goes to waste? This chapter will look first at the general principles that apply to the use of straw as fuel. The second section of the chapter describes actual practical examples of straw being used for fuel at a number of sites for agricultural, horticultural and domestic purposes. Thirdly, an estimate will be attempted of the possibilities that seem to be open for a greater use of straw as a source of fuel energy.

SOME GENERAL PRINCIPLES

The Energy Value of Straw
The energy or heating value of straw can be expressed in various ways. It can be expressed in terms of the calorie—a commonly used measurement of energy related to the amount of energy or heat required to raise the temperature of one gram of water by one degree centigrade—or in terms of the British thermal unit (Btu). However, it is intended here to use the standard international metric system wherever possible under which energy ratings are expressed in terms of megajoules (MJ) per kilogram (kg). The following simplified conversion table can be used to convert three commonly used measurements of energy into megajoules, within an accuracy of about 5%, for quick calculations.

Table 10. Conversion table for energy units

1000 British thermal units	1 MJ
240 calories	1 Btu
1 kilowatt hour (kWh)	3.6 MJ

Dry straw has an energy value of about 15 MJ per kg. The seven million tonnes of straw that are at present annually wasted or burned in the United Kingdom therefore contain approximately 105 thousand million MJ—or, to use the standard prefix which shortens the term, 105 TkJ. The total amount of energy used in agricultural and horticultural production in the United Kingdom has recently been estimated to be as shown in the following table.

Table 11. Primary energy consumed in United Kingdom Agriculture and Horticulture

	TkJ
Solid fuel	4
Petroleum	85
Electricity	33
Fertiliser	84
Agrichemicals	1
Machinery manufacture	52
Feedstuff processing (off farm)	53
Buildings, materials, etc.	23
Miscellaneous	28
TOTAL	363

Note. It is estimated that one-quarter of the petroleum is used for glasshouse heating.

In addition to the energy used in the agricultural and horticultural industry proper, there is the requirement for domestic hot water and central heating on farms. The extent of this requirement is not known accurately but, on the basis of 220 kWh, or 800 MJ, per day for two hundred days for a total of 250,000 farm houses and cottages for the whole country it would amount to around 40 TkJ.

It can therefore be seen that the energy lost through the wastage or field burning of straw in the United Kingdom represents a high proportion of the total energy used in the industry. It is equally clear from the above table that the possibilities for substituting straw are limited to only a few of the energy-consuming items. Before going on to consider where straw can economically compete with other fuels used in agriculture, it is necessary to look in more detail at some of the characteristics of straw as fuel.

The Comparative Heating Values of Fuels

The amount of energy or heat in different fuels is set out in the following table.

Table 12. Energy values of straw and other fuels

Material	MJ per kg
Straw (at 15% moisture)	15
Wood (at 15% moisture)	15
Good coal	30
Fuel oil	40–45

Straw has about half the energy or heating value of a good sample of coal and rather more than a third that of fuel oil.

Density

Another important characteristic of fuels is their physical density; Table 13 compares a number of different fuels in terms of their estimated average density in kilograms per cubic metre.

The advantage of the denser fuels is that they take up less storage space, can normally be burned in smaller furnaces, are

Table 13. The density of straw and other fuels

Fuel	Density in kg/m^3
Straw bales	100
Compressed straw bales	300
Dry timber	500
Coal	650
Straw pellets	650
Fuel oil	900

easier to transport and convey and can generally be stoked more quickly and easily.

Stoking and Combustion Characteristics

Straw in bales is inconvenient to stoke. Small bales must often be placed in the furnace by hand but large bales must be stoked mechanically, usually by tractor-mounted loaders.

Baled straw also has unsatisfactory combustion characteristics. The loose straw on the outside of bales flares up quickly but the middle of the bale, as it becomes surrounded by ash, tends to smoulder unless the draught is suitably adjusted. Although forced draught can partially overcome this problem, in furnaces whole bales tend to give uneven heat. The straw combustion characteristics are greatly improved if it is milled or chopped or if it is briquetted or pelleted so that it can be conveyed mechanically in thermostatically controlled amounts into the combustion chamber.

Cereal straw has a high silica content—as much as 6 per cent for wheat straw—and this can fuse at high temperatures to form a glassy slag which is difficult to clear from furnaces. The silica content of oilseed rape straw is much lower and nearer to that of wood. A good feature of straw is its low sulphur content; straw commonly contains around 0.05 per cent of sulphur while coal contains about 1 per cent. This is important because it reduces the likelihood of boiler corrosion and means that the smoke from straw-burning furnaces is much less polluting than smoke from coal.

The Effect of Species and Variety

So far as energy rating is concerned there are negligible differences between the straws of the three main cereals. Oilseed rape straw has the same gross energy content as the cereal straws, but its more open, woody nature allows it to burn better. This characteristic, along with its low ash content, makes oilseed rape straw popular as a fuel for straw-burning boilers. Wheat straw usually contains about twice as much silica as barley or oat straw.

The Effect of Moisture Content

The moisture content of straw has the most important influence on its value as fuel. In fact the useful energy developed from it is inversely proportional to its moisture content, as shown in figure 7. Part of the reduced value per kilogram of damp straw is due simply to the weight of the water but in addition there is the loss of energy taken up in driving off the water as vapour—the latent heat of vaporisation. The diagram shows clearly the steep falling off of nett energy value as the moisture content of the straw increases. All those who have used straw as a fuel

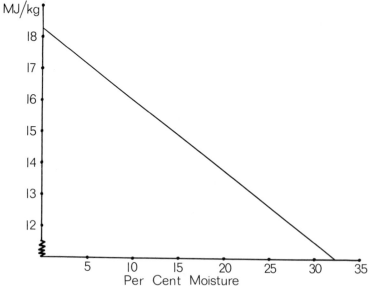

Fig 7. Approximate heating value of straw related to its moisture content (assumes 18.4 MJ/kg in the dry matter and 2.26 MJ/kg latent heat of vaporisation of water).

emphasise how important it is to harvest and store straw for fuel in the driest possible condition.

The 'Home-produced' Factor
One feature of straw as a fuel on the farm which is often mentioned by farmers is that it is a commodity under their own control—a considerable advantage in times when supplies of fuel from outside are subject to interruption.

The energy cost of collection
It is sometimes suggested that the cost of baled straw will increase in line with the increase in the price of oil because of the high energy cost of harvesting it. In fact, estimates made in the United Kingdom and abroad of the energy used in collecting straw in the field, including both fuel and the energy element in the machinery cost, range from 1½ per cent to 3 per cent of the energy in the straw. This means that increases in oil prices should be reflected only to a minor degree in the cost of energy in harvested straw.

PRACTICAL ASPECTS OF STRAW AS A FUEL

The Siting of Furnaces
Because of the size of the fire box and the bulkiness of the fuel, special provision has to be made for the siting of most of these installations.

Some farms have very convenient adjacent buildings or lean-tos which provide enough space for both the furnace and a reasonable supply of bales. Usually storage space for a minimum of one week's straw requirement should be immediately to hand. The furnace itself should be separated from the available supply of straw by a solid partition in order to reduce a fire hazard which arises, particularly when the furnace is cleared of ash. It is important that the area around the furnace should be kept scrupulously swept.

Some farmers have built lean-to boiler houses against their farmhouses. This reduces to a minimum the need for additional piping, but it has in some cases led to difficulties in providing a suitable flue. With early models there were problems with draught and smoke proved to be a nuisance, so that it was important to place the furnace and flue in a position providing the best conditions for draught and the least likelihood of nuisance from smoke. With later models, incorporating fan-assisted draught and greater combustion efficiency, these considerations have become less important.

A more important factor in many cases is the siting of the boilerhouse so that it can best serve several purposes. As will be shown in a later section, efficiency of combustion and convenience of operation may be best obtained with furnaces of large output, capable of supplying heat to more than one house on a farm, and perhaps also to workshops, dairy and glasshouse, or to dry grain or for other purposes. In such cases, farmers may have an existing building in a central position which can house the installation. More often it may be necessary to erect a house for the furnace. The energy produced, usually in the form of hot water, can be moved considerable distances in well-insulated piping which is generally laid underground, but this can be expensive.

It is always wise to seek the advice of reputable heating engineers about necessary pipe bores and lagging as well as other aspects of the installation.

A system which uses pelleted straw as a fuel will be described in a later section. With such a system many of the problems mentioned above will be avoided. Pellet-burning boilers, as developed in France, are no bigger or more expensive than most solid-fuel boilers. The fuel is clean and dense so that it should be possible to site such a system inside most farmhouses.

The Economics of Straw as a Fuel

The theoretical case for replacing mineral hydrocarbons with straw as a source of energy begins with a consideration of the cost of the energy in the fuels and the efficiency of combustion of that energy. The way in which this may be calculated is set out in Table 14 in which representative figures have been used; these figures will need to be adjusted according to circumstances. There can be large differences in the cost per tonne and energy content of the three fuels as well as in the efficiency of the furnaces.

This table takes no account of the capital cost of the furnace which tends to be greater for the straw-burners. The effect of the increased capital cost will depend upon the output of energy from the furnace. Thus for a furnace with an annual output of

Table 14. Relative Costs of Energy from Oil, Coal and Straw

Fuel	Cost per t £	MJ/t	Cost per '000 MJ £	Efficiency of Combustion %	Cost per '000 MJ (effective) £
Oil	140*	40,000	3.50	80	4.38
Coal	80*	30,000	2.66	70	3.80
Dry straw	20	15,000	1.33	60	2.22

* For small lots delivered to farm

100,000 MJ (effective), an additional cost of £1,000 as compared with an oil burner, written off over ten years at an annual interest rate of 15 per cent, will add an annual £200, or £2.00 per effective '000 MJ to the cost of energy. Adjustments of this nature will need to be made, according to circumstances, when comparing costs of straw-based with oil- or coal-based energy.

The other main factor to be taken into account in estimating the relative economic efficiency of straw and other fuels is the cost of labour in using the fuels and this is closely allied to convenience. This factor may be discounted to some extent on family farms but in other situations it may be crucial.

The economic efficiency of using straw as a fuel therefore depends mainly upon the price of the fuel as delivered into the combustion chamber, on the efficiency of combustion and on the labour cost/convenience factor. Great efforts have been made in recent years to make improvements in these various factors and the effect of such improvements is considered in the following paragraphs.

The Price of Straw Delivered for Fuel

The source of the straw greatly influences its effective price at the furnace. Farmers are obliged, when following the burning code or local by-laws, to clear the field headlands. The cost of baling these headlands may therefore be regarded as part of the cost of burning and this may effectively reduce the cost of the straw fuel in the furnace, assuming that there is no market for it. Some farmers may be able to store the straw in redundant buildings. If dry straw for fuel can be costed at the farm cost of baling and short-distance haulage to store, perhaps amounting to no more than £7.50 per tonne, then its competitiveness is greatly enhanced. Oilseed rape straw is difficult to burn on the field, and if it can be baled up this may be the cheapest and best way of disposing of it; so that it, too, may be regarded as a very cheap fuel when transported only a short distance from the field.

Bale Compaction Machines

These machines are being developed to compress standard square bales to about one-third of their volume (Plate 7). These enable furnaces to be stoked at longer intervals, as well as making for cheaper transport and storage. However, this bale compression is expected to cost at least £5 per tonne and the compacted bales are unlikely to lead to greater straw combustion efficiency.

Straw Pelleting or Briquetting

This has been tried as a means of improving the economics of transport and storage, the convenience of stoking and the efficiency of combustion. In France a number of co-operative grass-drying plants are pelleting straw with a molasses-based binder to form a free-flowing fuel with a density of 650 kg per m^3. These pellets are stored in self-emptying hoppers and stoked automatically into boilers which can also use coal or oil as fuel (figure 8). There is thermostatic control of fuel input and the boilers are said to give a combustion efficiency similar to

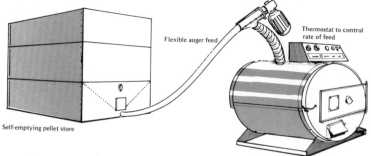

Fig. 8. French multi-fuel boiler adapted to burn straw pellets.

that of the best coal and oil burners. The price of the pellets at factory is currently quoted as £45 per tonne, so that these straw pellets are competitive with anthracite nuts at £120 per ton. The boilers being supplied for use with straw pellets and the storage hoppers cost little more than the equivalent oil- and coal-burning installations. A doubt remains, however, over the economics of production of the pellets. As an out-of-season activity at lucerne-drying plants, it may be possible to charge low overhead costs. If a factory had to be erected and manned solely for straw-pellet production it would be difficult to achieve profitable production at a price of £45 per tonne in the United Kingdom.

Big-bale Boilers

Big bales present the opportunity of moving large blocks of energy easily and economically (Plate 18). Thus one 350 kg big bale can be moved by tractor fore-end loader into a sufficiently large boiler in one operation and, provided it is dry, supply at 60 per cent efficiency, some 3150 MJ equivalent to 875 kWh or enough to heat a very large farmhouse for about a day. However, a boiler large enough to accommodate a big bale is

18.
One million Btu boiler being stoked with big round bales by fore-end loader.

expensive and requires a great deal of space. The bales themselves are relatively cheap to make but are expensive to store and keep dry.

Automatic Stoking

Attempts to automate the stoking of straw go back to the last century. There is an interesting account of systems in use over one hundred years ago in the *Journal of the Royal Agricultural Society of England,* Volume X, 1874, entitled 'Report from the Agricultural Features of the Vienna Exhibition 1873' by John Wrightson, Professor of Agriculture at the Royal Agricultural College, Cirencester. The great names of agricultural engineering of the time—Clayton and Shuttleworth, Ransomes, Sims and Head and Garretts of Leiston—were all concerned in developing straw-burning boilers and detailed drawings of the systems are shown in the Journal.

The Ransomes stoking system consisted of two teethed rollers turning (it was said) at 48 rpm, drawing long straw into the combustion chamber. The rollers were hand-turned until there was a head of steam, after which they were driven by a pulley from the machine. The silica in the straw was a problem in those days with a hand-operated rake being used to 'break up the siliceous crust deposited in the grate bars'. Regarding the efficiency of these nineteenth-century boilers, it was stated by Professor Wrightson that, 'in one case (i.e. for threshing) 20 cwt of straw was equal to 9 cwt coal', indicating that they were achieving approximatedy the two to one ratio in the quantities of the two fuels that one would expect to provide similar energy, given equal efficiency of combustion. Recent attempts at automated stoking (other than the methods described above using pellets or big bales) have approached the problem in a different way. They involve breaking up the straw and then blowing, augering or ramming it into the combustion chamber.

In the United States trials have been carried out on a system in which straw is hammer-milled to pass through 3 mm and 5 mm screens forming a straw dust which can be blown into suitably adapted boilers. The dust fired well in tests but it was found that low ash fusion temperatures led to heavy, glassy deposits of silica in the firebox. This method has the further disadvantage that the pulverisation of the straw is itself expensive in energy and there has been no commercial development of this system.

Other systems developed in recent years in Europe involve a much coarser breakdown of the straw, with a correspondingly lower demand for energy. There have been three main techniques employed. In the first the straw is chopped and blown into a large storage bin from which it is augered into the furnace. A second method employs a ramp up which bales are moved automatically to a toothed drum which shreds the straw so that it can be augered into the furnace. A third technique also conveys bales along a ramp, at the end of which a guillotine slices off a portion of the bale which is then rammed through a pipe into the furnace (Plate 19).

In the first of these methods bales have to be placed in the hopper of the chopping machine, but the chopping operation may be done at intervals, depending on the capacity of the storage bin and the demand for fuel. In the second and third models the bales have to be placed by hand on to the ramps leading to the shredder or guillotine, but provided there is sufficient space, a suitable length of ramp can be installed to ensure that enough bales are in position to ensure automatic stoking for at least ten hours.

In all three cases the rate of stoking is thermostatically controlled and there are safety devices designed to control any possible burning back. In all cases there is fan-assisted draught and tests have confirmed that these automated stoking systems give a greatly improved efficiency of combustion, perhaps double that of the first generation of straw-burning furnaces which used whole bales. Efficiencies in excess of 60 per cent are quoted for the most up-to-date furnaces. These automatically stoked furnaces in fact burn rather like gas furnaces with a more even output of heat than bale burners, with comparatively little smoke and less ash. Owing to the high temperature of the furnace, there is a tendency for the silica in the ash to fuse and the furnace walls may need to be lightly scraped down when the ash is removed.

These automatic stoking systems are still in the stage of development but they show promise of overcoming the problems of low efficiency and inconvenience of stoking associated with the earlier straw burning stoves. However, these improvements

19.
Automatic stoking attachment. Conventional bales are drawn down the track to a guillotine which cuts off a slice which is then rammed horizontally into the combustion chamber.

are achieved at some cost. An automatic stoking system may well add at least £5000 to the cost of the boiler. If the furnace is a large one with an output of, say, 500 MJ per hour, and if this output is used for most of the year, it may be possible to justify the additional cost. The annual charge to write-off £5000 at 15 per cent interest, over ten years, for instance, is £1000; for a boiler with a utilised output of 1 million MJ per annum, this would add a cost of £1 per thousand MJ.

There is also an electricity cost to be taken into account with these automatic systems. Employing a chopper-blower and auger system might be expected to add around £5 per tonne to the cost of the straw fuel. The other two systems demand less energy and it is claimed that the guillotine-ram method adds approximately £2 per tonne in electricity cost—as calculated at the time of writing—or £0.21 per 1000 effective MJ at 60 per cent efficiency of combustion.

One other system of simplifying stoking which is being tried is the magazine method. In this bales are placed in a vertical magazine down which they are fed by gravity into the combustion chamber. As the bales burn away, more slide down and the magazine is refilled (ideally from a loft), as required. The simplicity of the system is attractive but only one model of this type has been installed in the United Kingdom at the time of writing and it has yet to be proved reliable.

General Improvement in Boiler Design

Apart from the improved stoking and forced draught systems mentioned above, heat transfer systems in boilers have been improved and better materials and construction, improved flue design and the reuse of hot flue gases in the so-called two- and three- pass boilers have all contributed to improved efficiency in the latest generation of straw-burning boilers.

Some Effects of Adjustments to Costs and Combustion Efficiency on the Economics of Straw as a Fuel

The cost per 1000 effective MJ as shown in Table 14 will obviously be changed as costs per tonne of the fuel, or its quality or the efficiency of its combustion are altered. The capital cost of the boiler also has to be taken into account. The following are examples of the effect of changes in these factors.

(a) *Reducing the price of straw fed* into the boiler to £7.50 per tonne leads to a reduction in the cost per 1000 effective MJ at 60 per cent efficiency, to £0.83—less than one-quarter of the cost of using oil.

(b) On the other hand, *increasing the moisture content of straw* from 15 per cent to 27 per cent, and thus reducing its heating value to some 12 MJ/kg will increase the cost of energy produced by one-third.

(c) *If the price of straw is increased* to £45 per tonne by pelleting and at the same time combustion efficiency is increased to 75 per cent, the cost per 1000 effective MJ increases to £3.75.

(d) *Increasing the efficiency of a boiler* will reduce the cost per 1000 effective MJ. But, assuming that the more refined boiler required to achieve this improvement costs an additional £1000, and writing this off over ten years at 15 per cent on a comparatively small domestic boiler, delivering 144,000 MJ per annum, there would be an additional cost of £1.39 per 1000 MJ.

(e) *Automatic stoking systems* as indicated above are expensive. They can hardly be justified economically for boilers of relatively small output, but as shown in the example previously quoted, for a boiler with a utilised output of 1 million MJ per annum, adding an automatic stoking system costing £5000 may be calculated to add £1.00 to the capital cost plus perhaps £0.21 to running cost per 1000 MJ. Such a system improves the efficiency of combustion as well as convenience of operation. An increase in combustion efficiency of 15 per cent in a furnace previously rated at 60 per cent reduces the cost per thousand effective MJ by 20 per cent.

Ash—Disposal and Value

The ash produced in a straw-burning boiler will often amount to about 8 per cent of the weight of the straw burned. The more efficient the boiler, the lower will be the proportion of ash. This ash accumulates and has to be removed, normally by hand. It is light and dusty and its regular, often daily, removal is a considerable chore. However, automatic devices for ash removal have now been developed for some models of straw-burning boilers. These devices include an auger which lifts the ash into a container for removal.

A limited number of analyses have been carried out on the ash from straw burners and the following table gives the averaged results from two such analyses.

Table 15. Fertiliser elements in straw ash, per cent of dry matter (average of two Oxfordshire samples)

P_2O_5	K_2O	Mg	Ca
4.13	9.93	1.22	6.74

Ash with this analysis is quite a good source of potash and also contains appreciable amounts of phosphorus and magnesium. Suitably supplemented with nitrogen, it would be useful for many horticultural crops. Valuing the P_2O_5 at 36p per kg and the K_2O at 17p per kg, this sample would be worth

£31.75 per tonne. Clearing, transporting, spreading and storing small quantities of such ash at frequent intervals is a tedious task in the smaller furnaces. For instance, a boiler rated at 80-100 MJ per hour might use 50 tonnes of straw per annum and produce only about 4 tonnes of ash. However, arrangements have been made with a few of the largest straw-burning furnaces for the ash to drop through into a pit containing water from which it is evacuated into standard slurry tankers for spreading on the land.

A Straw-Fuelled Combine Harvester

Before going on to consider some present-day examples of using straw as a fuel, it is interesting and instructive to look back at a remarkable use of this source of energy almost a century ago. In 1886 George Stockton Berry, a farmer in the Sacramento valley of California, constructed the first self-propelled combine harvester, using a 25 hp steam tractor to propel the header and separator and a 6 hp Westinghouse steam engine to power the thresher. Both engines took steam from the same boiler which was fuelled by straw. The threshed straw from the separator fell into a chute and was delivered to a trailed platform just behind the boiler and was thence hand stoked into the furnace. An exhaust fan assisted the draught up the tall stack. A supply of straw was put on the trailer at the end of the day's work ready for the thirty-minute task of raising steam the next morning.

A number of these straw-powered self-propelled combines were made and a later model, shown in a photograph in *Power Farming* magazine, November 1980, had a 40-foot cut, with headlamps for night work, and was reported to have averaged 92 acres per day for the 1888 season.

Incidentally, the propelling steam tractor was unhitched from the harvester at the end of the season and used for ploughing, being fuelled from excess straw that was dumped on the land during harvest. This use of a renewable source is an extraordinary commentary on present-day calls for energy conservation.

PRACTICAL EXAMPLES OF THE USE OF STRAW AS A FUEL

Several thousand British farmers have installed straw-burning furnaces since the 1973 oil crisis. The following examples, for which the owners have supplied technical and economic information, illustrate how straw-burning systems can be adapted to particular circumstances. Some details are also given of a Danish municipal heating project.

1. Farm Domestic Hot Water and Central Heating
A farmer in North Oxfordshire has used a straw-burning boiler rated at 360,000 Btu (approximately 360 MJ) per hour for three seasons (Plate 20). The output is used to provide hot water and central heating for a large house and a bungalow as well as a workshop. There is no other form of heating available (apart from little-used open fires). Every harvest the plan is to set aside 4000 conventional bales (say, 70 tonnes) for use in the boiler; for some years this farm has grown about 16 hectares of oilseed rape which, assuming a yield of 200 bales per hectare, will provide about 3000 bales. The remainder of the requirement is obtained from the cereal crop. The rape comes early to

20.
A boiler which is used to provide central heating to two farmhouses and a workshop. Ash being removed. Note block wall between boiler and fuel store.

harvest and there is normally time to get the straw baled, using a flat 8 system on this farm, and carted before the start of the corn harvest. There is storage available on the farm and the straw fuel is costed at a low figure—£8.50 per tonne delivered to the boiler.

The boiler was put in an existing building between the farmhouse and the bungalow, and next to the workshop. It is convenient for stoking during the day as people move around the farmyard and there is adjacent storage for about one week's requirement of straw. The central heating is stopped on a time switch at night and restarted in the morning. The boiler is stoked, using three standard bales, at about 10.00 pm and is allowed to burn low, or even go out, during the night before being restoked early in the morning.

The boiler was installed complete with well-lagged underground piping to the houses and double-skinned chimney for an estimated £4000. This boiler probably had an efficiency of about 35 per cent but recent improvements, including an economiser which uses the flue gases to heat water in a second pass before going out through the chimney, and a fan for forced draught, have probably improved this efficiency to about 60 per cent at a cost of about £1000.

An additional benefit arising from these improvements is a considerable reduction in smoke emission. This farmer estimates that in an average year he replaces about 14,000 litres of fuel oil, which would cost about £1600 by some 70 tonnes of straw costing about £600. He considers the saving of about £1000 per annum to be a satisfactory return on the outlay of £5000 in spite of the extra work involved in stoking and the removal of ash. He values also his independence in the matter of fuel supply.

2. Domestic Hot Water, Central Heating and Grain Drying

A Gloucestershire farmer, farming in the Cotswolds at an altitude of about 1000 feet, installed a straw-burning boiler in a farm building in 1979, making use of an existing chimney. The boiler was of a simple, hand-stoked design with a rating of 250,000 Btu (250 MJ) per hour. The cost of the boiler was £1480. The output is used to provide domestic hot water and central heating for a large farmhouse, to heat a garage and a

21.
The heat exchanger used in conjunction with a 250,000 Btu boiler.

small greenhouse and to dry grain (average annual production
—520 tonnes). Connection to the house (65 m away), garage
and greenhouse and to the heat exchanger (Plate 21) for the on-
floor grain drier (30 m away), subsidiary electrical work,
header tanks and asbestos lining to the boiler shed are estimated
to have cost £3500. All the piping is of sufficient diameter to
deliver the required heat and is efficiently insulated. The grain
drier (Plate 22) had previously been operated from a 48 kWh
electric fan heater and the 250 MJ boiler has met this demand
for energy. However, an important feature of this installation is
that there is a back-up oil-fired furnace in case of emergency or
extra high demand.

22.
The grain store which is ventilated by air drawn through the heat exchanger shown in plate 21.

(Crown copyright)

Conventional bales will not keep the boiler fuelled all night and timber is used for this purpose if required. In practice it is found that on good combining days little or no heat or stoking is required, whereas on damp or wet days there is plenty of time available for stoking. If, after a combining day, the humidity rises in the evening, the boiler is stoked with straw and later at, say, 11.00 pm with timber which will last until 6.30 or 7.00 am next morning.

This farmer employs a contractor to bale sufficient of the driest straw available on his farm and he has adequate available covered storage space to accommodate his straw requirements. The contract charge for bales brought into store has been £15 per tonne. There is no accurate information on the efficiency of this boiler, but the farmer believes that he is saving annually about £1000 in drying costs as compared with electricity charges for the previous corn-drying system. He is unable to cost with accuracy the dead elm timber element in his fuel but he is satisfied that the system makes possible considerable economies compared with any alternative oil-burning system, and he has been prepared to accept the work of hand stoking.

3. Glasshouse Heating

A firm of nurserymen between Lincoln and Newark have used for two seasons a one million Btu (1000 MJ) big-bale boiler to provide under-floor heating for three-quarters of an acre of azaleas from October to the end of May. The boiler cost approximately £11,500 complete with chimney and installed. This boiler is fuelled with big round bales which are placed in it by a tractor and fore-loader. The normal procedure is to put two bales in the boiler early in the morning, three at about 5.00 pm and a further three bales later on in the night. A tractor-mounted shovel has been constructed for clearing out the ash—an operation which takes about forty minutes twice weekly. Some modifications have now been made to the boiler, including a baffle in the chimney and a larger fan, and it is now thought that there is a combustion efficiency of about 60 per cent.

About 1700 big round bales are used annually, 500 of them oilseed rape straw, each weighing about 150 kg, and 1200 of wheat straw, each weighing about 200 kg—a total straw consumption of 315 tonnes per annum.

The straw is provided free from a neighbouring farm on the understanding that it is removed immediately after combining. A contractor charges £1.40 per bale for baling and £0.60 per bale for transport—a total cost of £3400 or £10.79 per tonne. No charge is made for storage which is available on the holding.

Assuming that 90 tonnes of oil (efficiency of combustion 80 per cent) at £120 per ton, costing £10,800, would provide the same effective energy output as the 315 tonnes of straw (efficiency of combustion 60 per cent) costing £3400, there will be a gross saving of £7400 in fuel costs. With a ten-year write-off period and a 15 per cent rate of interest, the annual charge to write-off the cost of the straw-burning boiler, using standard amortisation tables, is £2300. The nurserymen do not know precisely how much they are saving by using straw instead of oil but it could well be around £5000 per annum. However, this figure takes no account of the greater inconvenience of using straw. Moving the big bales from storage to boiler takes time and requires the use of a tractor with fore-loader and a trailer which are strictly additional to the normal nursery requirement. An oil-burning boiler is also kept in reserve to top up heating requirements or in case of possible break-down of the straw-burning system.

The oilseed rape straw, though it burns well, is difficult to bale with the big round baler and the bales tend to break up. The grower has also had trouble with rats eating the polypropylene twine round big bales and this has led to considerable inconvenience. The bales are insured at a value of £5.60 per bale or £9520 in all.

4. District Heating

There is a Danish example of large-scale use of straw as fuel in a country town. Since 1980 the municipality of Svendborg has provided hot water to some 6000 people in the town by using three sources of energy:

	%
Household refuse (all the year)	30
Straw for nine months (excluding three summer months)........................	50
Oil (only during coldest weather)	20

The annual consumption of straw runs at about 14,000 tonnes which is purchased through contracts with ten contractors and seven farmers. The contract prices are on a sliding scale ranging from about £17 per tonne after harvest to £20 per tonne from March to April for straw delivered to the factory, at an average humidity of not more than 17 per cent. Svendborg is in an area where there are large amounts (perhaps 200,000 tonnes) of unwanted straw.

The make-up of a price of £18.50 per tonne has been estimated as follows:

	£/t
Bale	7
Transport on farm	3
Storage	2
Transport to power station	3
Farmer's profit	3.50

Clearly there are no wide margins for profit in supplying straw to the municipality at this price and it is not thought possible to achieve a profit at all if the straw is produced more than 45 km from the plant. Very large rectangular bales of high density have proved most suitable for this operation both for transport and for storing.

The straw is ground by 125 hp mills giving an output of 6 tonnes per hour of straw reduced to particles of 8-12 mm length. The output of these machines is seriously reduced if moisture content of the straw much exceeds 17 per cent. The ground straw is stored in silos from which it is augered out under thermostatic control and fed by blower into the boiler which consumes about 3 tonnes per hour—considered to correspond to about 1 tonne of fuel oil. The efficiency of the straw-burning boiler has been calculated by the Danish Association of Manufacturers of Boilers at approximately 78 per cent. About 5½ tonnes of ash are produced daily.

It is considered too early to make an accurate estimate of the economic result of the project. However, with heavy fuel oil costed at about £190 per tonne in Denmark (February 1981) there are clear possibilities for savings by straw. This is made even more likely because the Danish Governement subsidises the capital cost of fuel-saving installations. The project has been considered sufficiently promising for a further straw-burning power station of similar capacity to be put into service at Aarhus in Jutland in July 1981. However, it is clear that very great efficiency in collection, transport and storage will be required if the producer of this straw is to make a reasonable profit.

5. Onion Drying and Pack-house Heating

A radically different type of straw-burning furnace is being tested at The Ministry of Agriculture's Arthur Rickwood Experimental Husbandry Farm, Mepal, Ely, Cambridgeshire (Plate 23). This furnace is rated at 500,000 Btu (500 MJ) and a fan draws air over surfaces which are heated by the furnace gases for distribution through insulated distribution ducting. A thermostatically-controlled fan feeds air into the fuel chamber. Conventional bales are normally fed into the furnace by hand in batches of ten. The system cost about £1350 for the burner and

23.
Prototype straw-fuelled air heater installed at Arthur Rickwood EHF to dry onions and heat pack-houses.

flue, £3938 for ducting and insulation and £247 in electrical work.

The output of the furnace is designed to be used for onion drying in a 100-tonne onion store and to heat a workshop and packing houses. Straw has been costed at £10 per tonne and the system was budgeted to make a saving of £1000 over oil and propane costs after making allowance for additional labour in stoking, but not charging capital costs.

There has been considerable fluctuation in the heat output from this furnace, for which there is no hot water heat store, and, during the exceptionally cold weather of 1981-2 winter, the system proved incapable of delivering sufficient hot air to the pack houses. Smoke also leaked into the system.

The furnace required stoking at comparatively short intervals, taking ten standard bales at one loading. These, assuming that they contain 15 kg of dry straw, would supply an effective output of 500 MJ for only about 2½ hours at 60 per cent combustion efficiency. An experiment has been made using bales compressed to about one-third of their normal volume and this has been successful in reducing the frequency of stoking. However, the heat output continues to fluctuate as the bales alternately smoulder and flare up. It is thought that the problem of smoke leaking into the warm air system will be overcome by means of minor mechanical adjustments. It is also proposed to improve the efficiency of the air-heating system by recirculating the air from the heat exchanger instead of venting all the warmed air and drawing in fresh air at ambient temperature as at present. Much has been learned from the first season of operating this furnace and it is hoped that it will be functioning efficiently and achieving the planned economies in fuel costs during the coming winter.

Practical Possibilities for Using More Straw as Fuel

Of the list of items consuming energy in agriculture given in table 11, only the first three offer the possibilty for substitution by straw, and these account for 122 TkJ out of the total 363 TkJ. A high proportion of the 85 TkJ petroleum item is taken up by fuel for internal combustion engines and there is no prospect for straw substituting for this energy in the immediate future. Similarly the 33 TkJ used in the form of electricity is largely used to drive motors and no early economic means of replacing it by energy from straw can be foreseen. It is true that straw fuel could be used to raise steam. There have been suggestions in recent years that a new era of steam engines may be approaching as oil becomes prohibitively expensive. As mentioned earlier there were practical examples in the nineteenth century of straw fuelled steam engines and part of our huge straw surplus might have to be considered again as fuel for this purpose. However, it must be said that there is no real likelihood of this development in the near future.

The most promising use for straw as a fuel in the next few years must be as a substitute for oil (and the small amounts of coal and electricity) used in the provision of heat required in the industry. If we include heat used for domestic purposes on farms, the total amount of energy required for this purpose is considerable, perhaps as high as 70 TkJ, but for various reasons the practical possibilities for the use of straw for providing heat for agriculture and horticulture are very much less than this.

In all cases the cost of transport will be an important limitation to the economic use of straw as fuel. Moving straw any considerable distance from the farm on which it is produced is likely to add between £10 and £20 to the cost per tonne at present prices. With an absolute upper limit to its value as fuel set at half the price of good coal, a price penalty of this size is always likely to make straw uneconomic as a fuel. Densification, either into very compact bales or into cubes or briquettes would bring down the cost of transport but the process of compacting seems likely to increase the cost of fuel so much that it will become uncompetitive, unless cheaper methods of compaction can be devised.

Until cheaper methods of compacting straw into stable nuts or briquettes are found it must be assumed that straw will be competitive only on or very near to the farm where it is produced. With this limitation in mind, the following paragraphs consider some of the more promising purposes to which straw fuel might be applied.

Domestic Purposes

The first straw-burning boilers were installed in the United Kingdom for the provision of hot water and central heating to farm houses and farm cottages. Many of these boilers were in the 60-80 MJ range and were of crude design with poor draught control and low efficiency. All required hand stoking with conventional bales. There were problems with flues and smoke, and many farmers (or their wives, who frequently had to do the stoking) turned to using wood, often dead elm, as the main fuel, particularly overnight. The design of these boilers has now been improved to give better draught control and combustion efficiency.

There has been enough practical experience of the use of straw-burning boilers to show that, on cereal-growing farms, it is possible to save several hundred pounds per annum on heating oil, by using straw-burning boilers for central heating and hot water. At the present time this has to be done at the cost of considerable inconvenience in hand stoking and clearing ash. A number of farmers have sugared this pill by using the boilers to heat swimming pools—a purpose for which they are well suited. Other farms use their straw-burning boilers to heat non-commercial greenhouses and conservatories and even outdoor fish ponds. The hot water systems are often connected to farm cottages and to garages and workshops.

There are estimated to be a few thousand straw-burning boilers already in use for domestic hot water supply on farms. Assuming that there are 40,000 cereal-growing farms in the United Kingdom which have a surplus of straw, and assuming that perhaps one-quarter of them would turn to straw-fuelled boilers, one can estimate that up to ten thousand such boilers might be used for this purpose in this country, consuming up to 500,000 tonnes of straw per annum.

Crop Drying

There are now several examples in the United Kingdom of the successful use of straw burning boilers for on-floor *grain drying*, as described in the previous paragraph. There are good possibilities for making considerable economies by substituting straw-heated water-to-air heat exchangers for electrically heated banks for this purpose. There is very limited experience so far in the use of straw-fuelled boilers for continuous driers, where higher sustained temperatures are needed but some of the latest and most efficient automatically stoked boilers are being tried for this purpose. Corn drying, coming mainly in the summer, can conveniently make use of equipment which is used for domestic and other purposes mainly in the winter—this may help to spread the heavy capital cost of automatically stoked boilers and so reduce the cost of the energy produced. It is difficult to estimate the possibilities for future expansion in the use of straw to fuel grain driers, but it is possible that up to half the farms which have a surplus of cereal straw and which might install a straw-fired boiler for domestic purposes could use the same equipment for grain drying. This would lead to some five thousand boilers, using a total of perhaps 50,000 tonnes of straw for grain drying per annum.

Furnaces using chopped straw have proved economically

successful for *grass and lucerne drying* in France. It is possible that straw could be used for grass drying in the United Kingdom where the cost of fuel oil is threatening to destroy this industry. There are some other minor forms of crop drying, such as *onion drying* for which straw could well prove competitive as a fuel. The total amount of straw likely to be needed for crop drying other than grain drying is limited, at most, to a few thousand tonnes per annum.

There are some allied types of drying for which straw is being investigated as a possible fuel. These include the *drying of malt*. Where maltings are situated near the areas of surplus straw production, there are distinct possibilities for straw being used as a substitute for oil or coal to dry the malt. Trials are also being carried out on the use of straw fuel for hop drying. The principles set out earlier will apply equally to these potential uses of straw and there appear to be possibilities for some economies in fuel cost in this way.

OTHER WAYS OF USING STRAW AS A SOURCE OF ENERGY

At the present time the only method of using straw as a fuel that is of practical importance is by the direct combustion methods described above. However, there are other possible ways in which the energy in straw might be exploited and the following are brief notes and comments on some of these possibilities.

Bacterial Digestion
Bacteria can be encouraged to digest straw by providing the right conditions, including sufficient moisture and nitrogen. In this way straw bedding under livestock is digested and heat is generated in the process. This heat appreciably warms the bedding and atmosphere in many stock buildings and is presumed to lead to more comfortable conditions and economy of feed in some cases. The same principle has been applied by horticulturists for centuries in using 'hot beds'. Similarly, cucumber growers use the rise in temperature in a straw-based substrate to encourage the growth of the crop.

Industrial Alcohol
The production of industrial alcohol from straw was the object

of research for many years. This was encouraged by Henry
Ford in the early days of the automobile because the internal
combustion engine is easily adapted to use this type of fuel. In
Brazil and some other countries large quantities of 'gasohol' are
made from sugar cane and starch. It has been known for many
years that fuel of this type can be produced from straw but there
is an inherent problem. This is that straw needs expensive pre-
treatment such as milling and hydrolysis to break down the
cellulose and hemi-cellulose into carbohydrates that are more
readily fermented. This puts it at an economic disadvantage
when compared with other possible raw materials such as
sugars or starches.

Methane
Straw has been considered as a material, usually in association
with animal manure, which can be broken down by anaerobic
digestion to supply methane, sometimes known as biogas.
However, it is now generally considered to be a hindrance to
methane production because it is slow to break down and
interferes with the flow of animal manure in the continuous
digestors that are now thought to be most suitable.

Pyrolysis
This is a process of subjecting straw to high temperature whilst
limiting the supply of oxygen, in order to transform the energy
in the material to gas or oil. Research has been carried out on
the process in the United States and in Europe, notably at the
Warren Springs Laboratory in this country. The evidence to
date shows that, although a useful yield of energy from the straw
can be obtained in the convenient form of gas or oil, pyrolysis
cannot competitively produce fuel from straw, given the present
energy price structure. In Warren Springs tests it was found that
in order to bring the reactor up to the necessary temperatures of
$500°C$ or $800°C$, it would be necessary to use the whole of the
energy derived from the reactor.

Producer Gas
This is the gas which was made in trailers behind lorries and
buses for use in their engines during the last war. There has been
limited research in the United States on the use of maize cobs

for the production of this gas, the object being to use the producer gas for use in internal combustion engines for corn drying. All that can be said here is that the process is feasible and may be worth some further investigation in this country.

Chapter 4

STRAW FOR FEED

FACTORS AFFECTING QUALITY

STRAW IS INHERENTLY of low feeding value when harvested fully ripe. It has poor metabolisable energy and negligible protein, and is seriously deficient in minerals and vitamins. Even the best types of fully mature straw, when fed without supplement to full appetite, cannot provide enough energy, protein, minerals and vitamins to maintain cattle and sheep in good condition. Nevertheless straw has often played an important part in feeding livestock.

Both the Russian and German armies, as they rolled across eastern Europe at the end of the last war, still relied heavily on horses to move their material. It was the time of the scorched earth policy and horse food was scarce but it is reported that the army horse keepers could often find a cottage whose thatched roof they would strip to give their hungry animals some bulky food to eke out a tiny ration of meal. Much more recently in the great drought of 1976, many thousands of cattle in the stricken livestock areas of France were kept alive by the importation of a million tons of straw from the region of La Beauce alone in an operation assisted by the French army.

However, it is not only in time of famine and war that straw is valuable as feed. It has a part to play in the rationing of most ruminants, as well as for horses and minor classes of stock such as goats and rabbits.

On many farms there are available several sorts of straw and it is worth considering how straw type and variety, as well as a number of other influencing circumstances, may affect its nutritional value. This chapter begins by considering the many factors, including mechanical and chemical treatments, that can change the feeding value of straw. The second half of the chapter looks at the use of straw in the practical rationing of different classes of livestock.

Species

Table 16 shows that there can be quite wide differences in the laboratory analyses of samples taken from the same species of cereal.

Table 16. Averages and ranges of nutritional values of 160 straw samples taken from ADAS Cereal Variety Trials in South-East England in 1975

SPECIES	D VALUE (per cent digestible organic matter in dry matter)		CRUDE PROTEIN per cent in dry matter	
	Average	Range	Average	Range
Winter barley	45.5	44–49	2.8	2.0–3.3
Spring barley	44.5	40–49	2.9	2.4–4.2
Winter wheat	38.0	36–43	1.9	1.6–2.8
Spring oats	41.0	36–48	not available	

There can be much wider variations than shown in Table 16; for instance in 1981 wheat straw digestibility values in South-East England have varied from as low as 29 to as high as 46. In a 1967 survey in South-West England twenty-one barley straws gave an average crude protein of 4.6 per cent, with a range from 2.9 to 6.5 per cent. It seems clear that so far as laboratory analysis goes there is great variation within the species. Spring oats used to be considered the best feeding straw, but this was based on experience at a time when spring oats were often harvested by binder at an immature stage. When oats are combine harvested the straw may be little better nutritionally than that of the other cereals. Spring barley straw is generally preferred for feeding purposes to winter barley or winter wheat straw, and it certainly tends to be softer and, as a general rule, rather better in analysis. However, certain samples of winter barley and winter wheat straw have given better laboratory analyses than some samples of spring barley straw. For younger cattle some wheat straw has definitely proved to be hard and indigestible in some instances and spring barley straw is much to be preferred. Attention is being paid in various countries in the world to the apparently wide range in digestibilty in various samples of straw, and research workers are looking for consistent reasons for this variability.

Variety

Cereal variety may be an important factor. Thus in 1980, and again in 1981, the spring barley variety Triumph, a short-strawed variety, gave D values as much as ten percentage points higher than other varieties such as Georgie and Koru grown in trials in South-East England. Triumph showed a similar superiority at three trial sites in northern England.

It may be unwise to draw very definite conclusions from the limited number of analyses that have been done; but differences as great as ten points in D-value, as found in these trials, are too large to be ignored. The possibility arises that straw quality may become a factor of economic importance in some areas when choosing cereal varieties.

Stubble Height

Height of cut has a definite effect upon the feeding value of the harvested straw. Straw feeders can often observe that cattle and sheep offered long straw tend to consume the top end first and to leave the butt ends in the trough. The analyses shown in Table 17 support this observation, although there is no direct relationship between crude fibre and digestibility in straw.

Table 17. Analyses of barley straw divided into top, middle and bottom cut

Cut	Crude protein per cent	Crude fibre per cent
Top third	4.0	36.9
Middle third	3.0	48.0
Bottom third	2.9	50.2
Average	3.5	45.0

Seasonal Effect

The season can affect the quality of straw in at least one way. There is good evidence from more than one source that a very hot dry spell of weather at the critical time can curtail the growth of grain and lead to the retention in the straw of more than the normal amount of carbohydrate. Thus, in 1975 the severe summer drought led to some exceptionally good analyses of straw.

Weathering

Delays in straw collection may also affect its nutritional value. Tests in several countries have shown that the composition of straw is changed if it is left in the field and rain wets it before it is collected. Cattle have done better in trials when fed straw that was baled immediately after combining than when fed straw that had been rained on.

On the other hand, straw feeders in Lincolnshire used to prefer old straw from the previous year to the new season's straw. No clear scientific explanation has been advanced to support that preference but it is worth remembering that microbial and enzymatic activity can continue in straw that has been harvested dry and there is a possibility that this activity could improve the nutritional value of the straw. The use of biological methods to improve the feed value of straw will be considered later.

Soil and Fertiliser Effects

There have been few trials in which the digestibilities of identical varieties have been compared at different sites. An interesting comparison of this sort was made in the North of England by ADAS in 1980 when nineteen varieties of spring barley grown on three sites (Northumberland, Cleveland and Cumbria) were compared. The Cleveland site gave a statistically significant higher digestibility of straw from almost all the varieties when compared with the Northumberland site. It is not known what caused the difference.

Exeriments in Ireland showed that barley straw from the first or second tillage crops after grass had a rather higher crude protein content than straw from crops grown after a longer series of cereals. The same trial showed that higher rates of fertiliser nitrogen tended to increase the crude protein content of the straw, though only to a small extent in crops grown after the longer runs of cereals, when higher nitrogen dressings gave the greatest increases in straw yields.

Proportion of Leaf and other Fractions in the Sample

There are clear differences in the analysis of different parts of cereal straw, as shown in Table 18.

Table 18. The composition of five fractions of the straw of spring barley (SB) and winter wheat (WW) at harvest 1977. The figures are percentages of dry matter and are the averages from two cultivars in each case.

Fraction	Crude protein		MAD* fibre		In vitro digestibility		Total ash	
	(WW)	(SB)	(WW)	(SB)	(WW)	(SB)	(WW)	(SB)
Nodes	3.6	2.7	45.2	48.7	38	39	7.9	5.1
Internodes	2.5	1.5	52.5	57.9	39	38	5.6	2.7
Rachis	3.7	3.4	49.4	43.3	36	42	3.9	4.5
Leaves	5.5	4.2	47.4	47.3	41	53	14.7	6.8
Chaff/awns	4.9	2.8	45.2	43.4	33	45	8.3	13.3

* Modified acid detergent

This table shows that the internodes—sometimes known as the pipes—of the straw tend to be low in protein and high in fibre and of lower feeding value than the leaf or the threshed ear (rachis). These differences could become of practical importance if the different fractions of the straw are separated out, as in whole-crop harvesting. It has been shown that the combings from combed wheat 'reed' for thatch have a better analysis than ordinary wheat straw, as might be expected from the higher proportion of leaf to internode in the combings.

Stage of Maturity

It was always considered that oats cut by binder when still slightly green gave straw of a higher nutritional value than if they were cut fully ripe. There is some good evidence that the fibre content of straw increases considerably during the later stages of ripening of cereal crops. In addition it is well known that the leafy part of straw may become brittle as the crop ripens in hot, dry weather, so that some of this leaf, which tends to be more nutritious than the stem, may be lost in the process of combining and baling. There is also evidence that the crude protein content of very early cut straw is perhaps 2 or 3 per cent better than that of later cut crops. Therefore, it seems that the straw of crops combined early will tend to be more nutritious than that of late-cut crops and this has been confirmed in some laboratory tests.

Effect of Disease

It is not certain what effect cereal diseases have on the nutritional value of straw. One effect of diseases like rust and mildew will be to make the straw dusty. Also, some diseases will reduce the proportion of nutritionally valuable leaf in the straw. One would expect the straw from disease-free crops to provide a better feed than that from diseased crops.

How To Choose The Best Straw For Feeding

If a farmer has several different straws which he can use for livestock feed it is worth while choosing carefully. It may make some difference to the performance of stock being fed appreciable quantities of straw if that straw has a D-value of, say, 49 instead of 29; energy intake would increase because of the higher D-value and also because animals would tend to eat more of the more digestible roughage.

To summarise the points made in the preceding paragraphs, a farmer is more likely to choose a nutritious type of straw if he observes the following points:

1. Spring barley straw is generally to be preferred.
2. Some varieties may be better than others—for example, Triumph spring barley—but more evidence of varietal difference is needed. In any case, choose a straw with plenty of leaf.
3. Crops cut at an early stage of maturity should have a higher D-value than when cut late.
4. A high stubble tends to give the best straw for any particular crop.
5. A bright, undiseased straw is to be preferred.
6. Do not allow the straw to be rained on.

It may well pay a farmer to have straw analysed when it is to form a considerable part of stock rations. Laboratory analysis should give a guide to choosing straw of better feeding value, providing the samples are properly taken. Ruminants can be expected to consume much more of a straw with a digestibility of 49 than they would of a straw with a digestibility of 29—as previously mentioned.

THE EFFECT OF TREATMENTS ON THE NUTRITIONAL VALUE OF STRAW

Mechanical Treatments

There is no evidence that chopping or coarse grinding of straw will increase its digestibility. However, this treatment does make straw suitable for use in mixer wagons or forage boxes. Tub grinding in particular gives a lacerated, fluffy type of straw which appears to be acceptable to cows and readily absorbs the molasses now used in complete diets. Also a greater proportion of surface area will be exposed to microbial attack. Chopping or coarse grinding converts straw to a state in which it can be mechanically conveyed to certain classes of stock. However, when fed to dry cattle or suckler cows, for instance, there is no evidence to suggest that chopping or grinding—which may cost at least £10 per tonne—will give profitable results.

There is some evidence that very fine milling of straw will break the lignin, wax or silica coating which interferes with the digestibility of the cellulose in the straw. However, such milling is very costly and there is no suggestion that it would be a profitable way of increasing digestibility. Digestibility might even be decreased because of faster rate of passage. There is evidence also that, if straw is milled to a fineness of 2 mm or less, it will lose its value as a fibrous food for ruminants with the consequence of reduced butter fats if such finely milled straw were fed as the sole source of roughage to dairy cows.

Sodium Hydroxide

It has been known since the end of the nineteenth century that the digestibility of straw could be increased by soaking it in a solution of sodium hydroxide. This process—known as the Beckmann method—was used on a large scale in Germany in the First World War and was used in several countries in the Second World War. It was capable of making an appreciable improvement in the organic matter digestibility of straw. However, it has serious drawbacks. It tends to be laborious even when partially mechanised, and soluble nutrients are washed out of the straw leaving an effluent which can cause

24.
A modern factory for treating straw with sodium hydroxide. (BOCM Silcock)

pollution. This alkali treatment has been recently modified to a semi-dry process in which the disadvantages of the old soaking method are avoided.

The semi-dry treatment usually involves an addition of about 4.5 per cent of sodium hydroxide weight for weight to the straw. In the *factory process* the straw is ground, mixed with alkali and pelleted (Plate 24). In the pellet press high temperatures and pressures improve the action of the alkali. After cooling, the pellets, which usually have a density in excess of 500 kg/m^3, are conveyed to storage silos. The D-value of the straw, as shown by in-vitro tests, is increased in this process by up to twenty units (up to 65 D) but feeding trials usually show a smaller improvement—perhaps up to fifteen units when the treated straw forms a large proportion of the diet. In fact, most of the factory-produced alkali-treated straw ('nutritionally improved straw') has been used by commercial feed compounders at inclusion levels of around 15 per cent. The pellets have the advantage of convenience for transport, conveying and processing in compound mills.

On-farm treatment can in theory be carried out with the aid of a watering can and a pitchfork. However, sodium hydroxide is a very dangerous chemical and mixing it with straw by hand is not recommended. Machines have been developed for on-farm use in which bales are shredded, sprayed with sodium hydroxide and passed through a chamber in which the alkali is mixed with the straw (figure 9). The treated straw is then put into a heap (Plate 25) in which heat develops and increases the action of the alkali. These on-farm treatments have generally given increases in D-value of around fifteen units when they are properly carried out.

Does it pay to treat straw with sodium hydroxide? Both the factory and on-farm treatments have been given an extensive trial in the United Kingdom over the past five years. As a rule of thumb it may be said that a good sample of treated straw can be valued at 60 per cent of the price of the barley. If barley can be purchased at £100 per tonne, or can be provided on the farm at a similar figure, treated straw can be worth £60 per tonne. The cost of treating straw with alkali varies greatly according to the throughput of the machines but, with the alkali costing about £14, the whole treatment is unlikely to cost less

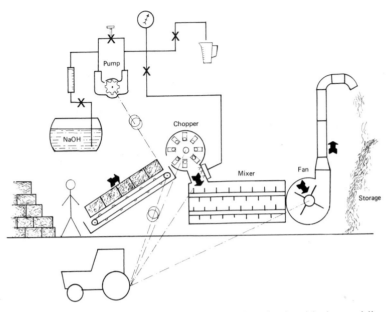

Fig. 9. Method of treating straw with sodium hydroxide by mobile machine.

25.
A mobile machine, equipped for mechanical loading into tub grinder for sodium hydroxide treatment.

(Power Farming)

than £30 per tonne. With dry straw costed in at £20 per tonne, the treated product will cost £50 per tonne and, on some farms, this may be an economic price for a reliable roughage.

Feeding trials show that the advantages of treating straw with sodium hydroxide are comparatively small when the treated straw forms only a small proportion of the ration. However, when large amounts of treated straw are fed to cattle the high sodium content results in increased urination and means that up to 30 per cent more straw bedding may be required.

The verdict on the sodium-hydroxide treatment of straw at the present time must be that there are comparatively small returns from on-farm treatment. If coarse grain prices increase further, the case for straw treatment will improve but, at present prices, a satisfactory ration for ruminants can be formulated more cheaply by increasing the level of supplementation of barley or other high-energy food, while paying attention to the nitrogen requirement in the form of rumen degradable protein.

Ammonia
The interest has shifted during the past few years to ammonia as a chemical for treating straw, mainly because it has the advantage over sodium hydroxide of improving the crude protein analysis of straw as well as its digestibility. Ammonia treatments usually involve treating straw with ammonia at 3½ per cent weight for weight. Effectiveness drops off rapidly if less than 3 per cent is used. Three methods are in use:

1.   Injection of anhydrous (pure, gaseous) ammonia into stacks covered with plastic sheets.
2.   Injection of aqueous ammonia (usually a solution of 28-35 per cent of ammonia in water) into stacks covered with plastic sheets (Plate 26).
3.   Injection of anhydrous ammonia into sealed metal containers, or 'ovens', in which heat is applied (Plate 27).

The speed of reaction of ammonia with straw is greatly affected by temperature as indicated in table 19.

There is some evidence that best results require the straw to have a moisture content of between about 8 and 20 per cent. Provided the processes are carried out efficiently there seems to

26.
Cattle on an Oxfordshire farm being fed ammonia-treated straw from
the stack in the background.

(Crown copyright)

27.
Ovens for ammonia treatment of straw.

(Bill Butterworth)

be little difference in their effectiveness if the three methods are allowed sufficient time.

Some increases in digestibility and crude protein content by the anhydrous method have been as shown in table 20.

Table 19. Time required for ammonia treatment of straw at different temperatures

Temperature	Time Required
less than 5°C	More than 8 weeks
15–30°C	1–4 weeks
over 90°C	Less than 24 hours

Table 20. Increases in D-value and crude protein content of barley and wheat straw by treatment with anhydrous ammonia

		Crude Protein per cent of dry matter	D-value
Barley	untreated	3.5	44
	treated	8.4	59
Wheat	untreated	4.0	49
	treated	8.0	62

Treatment in stacks with aqueous ammonia, mainly in the north of England, has given results which on average are only about half as good as those shown in table 20, with great variation from farm to farm.

The running costs of these systems do not differ greatly. The stacks are usually of about 20 tonnes, to suit the dimensions of the plastic sheets which are supplied by the contractor who provides the ammonia. The total cost of ammonia, at around £15, and the sheet, works out at £20 per tonne or rather less if the sheets can be used more than once. The cost of the oven depends upon its capacity; smaller models holding between 750 and 1000 kg cost about £4000 and other models costing about £8500 can take up to four 600 kg bales. With normal amortisation charges, the cost per tonne of straw treated in ovens, including the cost of electricity and hire charge for the anhydrous ammonia container, may be the same as, or rather less than, the cost of treatment in stacks using renewable sheets, provided the full output of the oven is obtained over the season.

The advantages and disadvantages of the systems of ammonia treatment may be summarised as follows:

	Stack Treatment	Oven Treatment
Advantages	Low capital cost. Amount unlimited in units of about 20 tonnes.	Reliable results. A routine daily job can be done throughout the year.
Disadvantages	Less reliable. Plastic sheets liable to damage. High labour requirement. Treatment best done at harvest time, when labour is scarce.	High capital cost. Mechanical troubles. Must be near electricity. Output may not match herd size. Much hand labour is needed if conventional bales are used, but can be mechanised.

It is advisable to choose the best straw available for ammonia treatment. Even though inferior straw may show the greater percentage increase in digestibility, the end result will not be as good as when better straw is treated. It is claimed that good ammonia-treated straw is equivalent, so far as energy and crude protein are concerned, to moderate hay, and this seems to be borne out in practice. However, the treated straw remains very deficient in minerals and vitamins, and it is essential when feeding a high proportion in the diet to add a mineral- and vitamin-rich supplement.

It is still too early to say whether ammonia-treated straw will find a permanent place on British cereal/livestock farms. The oven method has given the most consistent results in the United Kingdom so far but mechanical faults have arisen in a few cases. At present one weakness in ammonia treatment systems is that about two-thirds of the ammonia used in the treatment is lost to the atmosphere. If economic methods can be found to avoid this wastage the cost of treatment will be brought down. It is also possible that cheaper ovens can be made to suit individual farm needs. If a reliable hay substitute can be produced at a price of, say, £35 per tonne, and perhaps release grassland for more profitable crops, then the system may have a future. It has also to be emphasised that ammonia gas, though perhaps not as dangerous as sodium hydroxide, is extremely unpleasant when it escapes in a concentrated gust and could be very dangerous in certain situations.

Other Chemical Treatments

Among other chemicals which have been mixed with straw in order to improve its feeding value are calcium hydroxide, sulphur dioxide, ozone and urea. Calcium hydroxide has the advantage that it is much safer to handle than sodium hydroxide but it is slower to act. Straw treated with 5 per cent calcium hydroxide and ensiled for three weeks only showed an increase in digestibility of about 10 per cent. Urea treatment in which the production of ammonia from the urea is an essential step, has shown some promise but this process requires a high ambient temperature in order to work well and it may be best suited to tropical climates. Neither sulphur dioxide nor ozone treatments show promise at present of being economic.

Biological Improvements

A number of different methods of improving the feeding value of straw by biological methods have been tried. These include growing fungi on straw and feeding a mixture of the two—which has been called mycofutter on the Continent. This method seems too unpredictable and it has not been taken up on a farm scale.

A more promising method would be to attack the straw with fungi which, through their enzymes, break down the ligno-cellulose complex and thus render the cellulose fraction of the straw more available to microbial action. Such fungi occur in nature and have been shown to work well, but only when the harmful microflora are kept away. This type of sterilisation is impossible to carry out economically on farms. The use of laboratory-produced enzymes in place of the fungi may enable the process to be speeded up and made more efficient. For the time being, however, there is no likelihood of commercial systems for enzymic improvement of straw becoming available in the near future.

A more practical method of achieving a similar result may be to stimulate the production of correct enzymes in the animals' own rumen. A farm system for putting this principle into practice has been worked out in Denmark and is known as the 'Strawmix' system.

The Strawmix System

Experimental work has suggested that it is possible to stimulate the growth in the rumen of bacteria which secrete the enzyme which digests cellulose—namely, cellulase. The aim is to formulate a ration which ensures:

a.   inclusion of an ingredient, such as sugarbeet pulp, which contains cellulose but with a low lignin content.
b.   addition of an easily available carbohydrate such as molasses, as an energy supply, and
c.   supplementation with available nitrogen, sulphur and other minerals known to be important in the enzyme breakdown of cellulose.

It is claimed that when straw is fed as a high proportion (at least 55 per cent) of a ration formulated according to the above principles, the digestibility is greatly improved and that straw in these conditions can have a metabolisable energy value as high as 10 MJ per kg—as good as the best hay.

This theory has been put to the test on a few British farms. One way has been to purchase the special machinery which chops the straw and intimately mixes it with the other ingedients in pre-determined proportions such as:

55 parts straw
25 parts beet molasses
15 parts dried beet pulp
5 parts premix containing non-protein nitrogen, vitamins and minerals.

The other method has been to use available chopping machinery and to mix the ration formulated along similar but not necessarily identical lines in a mixer wagon, or even by using a forage box.

Measurements are being carried out on some British farms at the present time but so far there is no reliable experimental evidence to demonstrate that the Strawmix system can achieve the claimed increases in digestibility and metabolisable energy, under normal farm conditions. However, it can be said that on a few farms satisfactory milk yields have been obtained by using rations of the Strawmix type. The system is still under trial and it is too early to say whether it will enable more straw to be used profitably in dairy herds.

Mixing with Silage

There is no reliable evidence that the digestibility of straw can be improved by mixing it with silage. However, there are ways in which mixtures of both untreated and chemically-treated straw with silage may show advantages.

Sodium hydroxide treated straw has been successfully ensiled between layers of grass silage for later self-feeding. In another farm trial ammonia-treated, forage-harvested straw was placed below maize silage in a large walled clamp which was cut out for forage box feeding to beef cattle. Both these arrangements had the advantage of consolidating the chopped treated straw and so reducing the storage volume.

A third interesting system makes use of straw to absorb effluent from high-quality, direct-cut grass silage. There is evidence that silage made from direct-cut young grass has a better feed value than similar silage made from wilted grass and that feeding it will give better milk yields from dairy cows. A serious drawback to any system of ensiling fresh cut young grass has been the great amount of effluent that is produced. Trials in the Midlands have shown that straw bales may be used to absorb effluent from silage while, in so doing, their own feeding value is enhanced.

Conventional straw bales are packed on their side in a layer on the floor of a pit or clamp silo. It is recommended that an acidifying additive be applied to the bales as well as to the ensiled grass. There is no difficulty in placing the grass over the bales if a ramp is formed at the edge and the grass is pushed forward with a buckrake over the bales. The tractor can then run over the grass in the normal way when filling a silo. Further layers of bales may be put in position as the clamp is filled from front to back. Experience so far indicates that the bales are not greatly compressed by the overlying silage.

Three bales on edge will support a column of silage 1½ m high that will weigh approximately 1 tonne. These bales will absorb around 180 kg of effluent. 1 tonne of fresh grass containing 15 per cent of dry matter may be expected to give between 150 and 300 kg of effluent.

Straw which has absorbed silage effluent in this way has been analysed with the result shown in table 21.

Table 21. Analysis of straw bales used to absorb effluent from direct-cut young grass silage placed above them.

pH	Dry matter %	ME MJ/kg	Crude protein %
4.3	25.2	8.3	7.3

The most convenient way to feed the treated straw may be by self-feeding—for this the bands should be cut and removed and this may need to be done when the bales are positioned.

In practice it had been found that cattle find the soaked straw very palatable.

This system of ensiling straw with young, fresh cut grass is still in the development stage; a number of farmers will be trying it in 1982 and this will provide more information as to its possible future application. Wilting silage has an advantage in reducing the weight of material to be carted to the silo, but direct cutting avoids losses from transpiration, and perhaps from damage by the weather, while reducing soil contamination. If the use of straw to absorb effluent proves successful, the system may be taken up on a wide scale and large quantities of straw could be used in this way. A mixture of sugar beet tops ensiled over straw bales could perhaps provide valuable feed for beef cattle and there is scope for further on-farm trials along these lines.

The Use of Urea-Based Supplements
Urea has been fed with straw with the aim of providing nitrogen

in a readily degradable form to stimulate the activity of bacteria in the rumen which can break down the cellulose. Urea does not itself directly alter the D-value of the straw.

Proprietary supplements based on urea and including minerals, trace elements and vitamins are available either as solid block licks, or in liquid form using molasses as the carrier. Liquid supplements may be fed as a lick from a special dispenser or it can be applied simply through a watering can to the straw. By increasing the rate at which the straw is broken down by microbial action, such supplements appear to increase the animal's appetite for the straw. A considerable number of farmers have fed urea-based supplements with straw and some Experimental Husbandry Farm trials have shown that for both cattle and sheep the system improves intake of straw and liveweight gains. When supplementing straw with urea-based supplements it is essential to ensure that the diet also contains readily digestible energy sources and minerals, especially sulphur.

The cost of the supplement when licks are used is rather unpredictable because the stock may take more than is intended. When the supplement is watered on to straw at the recommended rate the cost at present prices is about £15 per tonne treated.

The analysis of the straw plus supplement, when correctly fed, can be compared in nutritive value with that of low-quality hay. Straw treated and fed in this way should not provide a large proportion of the ration for animals from which high production is expected. For preference it should be fed to suckler cows, store stock or to milking cows in the later stages of lactation.

The economics of feeding straw with urea-based supplements must depend greatly upon the availabilty of hay or silage of a similarly low digestibility at moderate to low cost. The system will show to advantage when hay and silage are expensive or scarce and when good feeding straw is abundant and cheap.

STRAW IN LIVESTOCK RATIONS

Having described the nutritive value of the various types of straw and the effect that certain factors, including chemical and other treatments, can have on that value, the following section considers how straw in various forms can be introduced into practical livestock rations. Rations for livestock have been studied scientifically for more than a century but it has to be admitted that successful stock-feeding remains something of an art and, particularly in the case of straw, animal nutritionists prefer not to be dogmatic about precise feeding values. Much depends on the age and breed of the animal, the way the straw is introduced into the ration and the nature of the feeds fed with it. Furthermore, as has already been shown, there can be unexpectedly wide variations in the feed value of different straw samples. The following examples of the use of straw in practical rationing assume average straw D-value of 40-45 and a crude protein of between 2 and 4 per cent unless otherwise stated.

Cattle

In a standard textbook on livestock published at the end of the last century the following daily ration was set out for *fattening beef cattle* to put on 6.5 kg per week for finishing at around 500 kg liveweight:

Average	1.4 kg cake	both beginning at 0.9 kg and ending
	1.4 kg meal	with 1.8 kg per day.
	38 kg roots	
	8 kg straw	

A ration to give an average gain of about 6.5 kg per week and feeding good straw, published in a modern Ministry of Agriculture, Fisheries and Food advisory leaflet is given in table 22. In this table figures in brackets show adjusted amounts to be fed if the quality of the straw is poor.

Table 22. Ration for fattening cattle

Weight of animal kg	Good straw kg	Beef compound feed (14% crude protein) kg
300	3.4 (2.8)	4.4 (4.9)
400	4.8 (3.8)	5.0 (5.7)
500	6.2 (5.0)	5.6 (6.6)

Assuming a dry-matter content of 10 per cent and a crude protein content of about 10 per cent in the roots, the two rations, worked out on a dry-matter basis, are quite similar except for the greater quantity of straw in the older ration. Straw tends to be costive and the roots would counteract this.

Experiments in Scotland reported in 1918 showed that cattle with an average weight of rather less than 500 kg finished satisfactorily over the three- to four-month period to slaughter on an average daily ration of:

> Turnips/swedes 41 kg
> Oat straw 6 kg.

The cattle in this experiment gained in liveweight at between 0.58 kg and 0.65 kg per day over periods of between 94 and 120 days.

The above ration illustrates how good straw, supplemented with roots or compound feed, can provide production rations for fattening cattle. Suckler cows and store cattle can be fed rather greater proportions of straw in their rations.

For high-yielding dairy cows too much straw, especially in early lactation, would reduce the energy concentration of the ration and fail to support potential production. However, cows require digestible long fibre for satisfactory rumination and butter fat production, and a minimum amount of roughage should be fed for this purpose. ADAS leaflet 551 give the rations shown in table 23 for feeding good-quality barley straw to Friesian cows.

ADAS leaflet 551 stresses the importance of ensuring that all cows in the herd receive their proper allowance of both straw and concentrates. Where possible the herd should be divided into high-, medium- and low-yield groups so that their allowance of feed can be better controlled. In early lactation cows may not eat enough straw and it may be necessary to replace it with more palatable hay. It also has to be remembered that straw is a costive feedstuff and it will generally be best to feed other more laxative ingredients with it wherever possible. Furthermore a diet including much straw may be deficient in the pigments that impart colour to Channel Island milk, and some such diets may not provide the minimum of 3 per cent oil required for optimum

Table 23. Rations for a 600 kg Friesian cow per head daily

	STAGE OF LACTATION			
	Early lactation M + 30 kg milk	Mid lactation M + 20 kg milk	Late Laction M + 10 kg milk*	Dry late pregnancy*
Barley straw kg	6	6	6	6
Dairy compound feed kg†	16.5	11.5	9.5	5
Barley straw kg	6	6	6	6
Brewer's grains (ensiled) kg	10	10	10	6
Barley kg‡	5	5	4	3
Dairy compound feed kg§	8.5	4	2.5	–
Barley straw kg	6	6	6	6
Dried grass kg ◊	5	5	5	4
Barley ‡	2	2.5	2	1.5
Dairy compound feed kg§	10	5	3	–

*Allows for liveweight gain and growth of the foetus.

† Dairy compound to have a metabolisable energy (ME) content of 12.5 MJ/kg DM; 14 per cent crude protein and adequate minerals/vitamins.

‡Barley to be rolled or ground and include a mineral/vitamin supplement at the maker's recommended rate.

§Dairy compound to have a metabolisable energy (ME) content of 12.5 MJ/kg DM; 16 per cent crude protein and adequate minerals/vitamins.

◊Dried grass of good quality, D value 65 and 16 per cent crude protein. Animals yielding 30 kg milk or more many not eat the full allowance of barley straw, due to appetite restriction for dry matter, but 6 kg straw should be offered so the animals can select the most palatable material.

butterfat production unless ingredients are included that ensure this minimum. On the other hand, straw as a roughage may have an advantage because it provides a uniform contribution to diet which can be accurately supplemented throughout the lactation and thus avoid the fluctuations in nutrient intakes that are associated with some of the traditional feeding systems.

Suckler cows can make good use of the straw in their rations. For example, a housed 500 kg beef cow could be expected to maintain herself and supply the needs of an unborn calf on a ration of:

> Good straw 7 kg
> Concentrate (15% protein) 3½kg.

However, the concentrates need to be increased if the cattle are kept out of doors in severe weather, due to increased maintenance requirements. Cows with calves at foot and with no access to grass or silage will need an additional 2-3 kg of concentrate to allow for the production of 5-7½ kg of milk per day.

For *store cattle* or *replacement heifers,* when the aim is to achieve a liveweight gain of 0.5 kg per day the following rations are suitable:

Weight of animal kg	Good straw kg	Compound feed containing 17% protein
200	2.2	2.4
300	3.7	2.8
400	5.0	3.0

The Effect of Chemical and Mechanical Treatments of Straw on its Use in Rations for Cattle

The effect that chemical treatment of the straw can have upon ration formulation is illustrated by calculating its effect on one of the store rations given above. If treated with sodium hydroxide the digestibility of good straw may be raised from, say, 45 to 60 D-value and the energy value from 6.75 MJ per kg to 9 MJ per kg.

This means that a store animal weighing 400 kg requiring 5 kg of untreated straw plus 3 kg of 17 per cent protein cake, can theoretically obtain enough energy from 5 kg of treated straw plus 2 kg of cake. This ration would, however, be deficient in protein and would need to be supplemented with a degradable nitrogen source such as urea. There is some practical on-farm evidence that rations for store cattle can be cheapened in this way but it has been noticed that feeding a high proportion— more than 50-70 per cent on a dry-matter basis—of sodium hydroxide-treated straw in a ration leads to increased urination and up to 30 per cent more straw bedding being required.

If straw is treated with ammonia, to give an increase in ME from 6.75 to 9 MJ per kg and also an increase in crude protein from 3.5 to 8.5 per cent a ration of 6 kg of ammonia-treated straw and 1½ kg of 17 per cent protein cake, suitably supplemented with minerals and vitamins, should be adequate as a store ration. There is no increased urination or water consumption with ammonia-treated straw.

In practice, another effect of treating straw with sodium hydroxide and ammonia, and also with urea-based supplements, has to be taken into account. This is the increased intake of straw by the animal as compared with untreated and un-supplemented straw. This may allow greater reduction in the concentrate allowance in the ration than shown above, provided that the protein–mineral–vitamin allowances are maintained. This effect is illustrated in table 24 which shows how increased intake of straw following an improvement of 15 units of D value with an assumed increase in metabolisable energy from 6.3 to 8.5 MJ/kg enables a ration to be adjusted. The increased intake possible from treated straw has been allowed for in rations *3* and *4*.

Table 24. Rations for 350 kg bullock to gain at 0.7 kg/day

	(1) kg/day	(2) kg/day	(3) kg/day	(4) kg/day
*Untreated straw	4.7	–	–	–
*Treated straw	–	4.7	6.4	7.8
Barley	3.4	2.3	1.1	–
Protein concentrate (35% protein)	0.7	1.0	1.3	1.5

*Untreated and treated straw assumed to be 86% DM for comparative purposes.

As a result of the increased intake of straw made possible by improved D-value, ME and crude protein content following treatment with ammonia, it has been reported from Norway that steers in their second winter, at 1½-2 years of age, can be satisfactorily stored on an ad-lib ration of such treated straw, provided they receive the necessary supplement and minerals.

Farmers have tried out various treatments of straw for

feeding to dairy cows. Coarse grinding, usually with a tub grinder, makes it possible to mix straw in mixer wagons or to feed it through forage boxes. This grinding, particularly when the straw is mixed with molasses and suitably supplemented with crude protein, improves the intake of straw by high-yielding dairy cows. The chemical treatment of straw will improve both palatability and intake and the metabolisable energy of the straw, and enable a small reduction to be made in the concentrate element in the ration. Ammonia treatment should also allow some economy to be made in the amount of crude protein to be supplied by other ingredients.

Sheep

Sheep will eat about the same amount of straw, in relation to their liveweight, as cattle but they must have high-quality straw. An example from South-East England illustrates how good, untreated straw has replaced hay for feeding ewes on a mixed farm, thus using a by-product that would otherwise be wasted and releasing grassland for cash crop production. It is necessary to describe the system in some detail because its undoubted success on some farms depends upon careful attention to flock management.

The ewes which are due to start lambing in mid March to early April are brought in to a well-littered house in the first week in January. It is important that the ewes are in good condition at this time because there is normally some loss of weight in the week after housing as they adapt to the new ration. To ensure that the ewes do not suffer seriously in condition after housing it may be advisable to feed 0.25 kg of cereal per head per day for three to four days before housing. When ewes are housed good-quality clean straw is offered at 1½ kg per ewe per day but it can be decreased to about 1 kg per day at lambing. The ewes are fastidious feeders and will only eat about three-quarters of this allowance, picking out the best. The straw is fed in bales in low feed boxes and shaking up is not necessary. It is important that the straw be available continuously so the ewes can consume little and often, particularly when close to lambing, and thus avoid prolapse problems. The straw should be completely renewed each day.

A concentrate containing 12.5 MJ of metabolisable energy

per kg of dry matter and 16 per cent crude protein with suitable mineral/vitamin supplementation should be fed at rates shown in table 25. This compound could take the form of eight parts cereal to two parts soya bean meal with a sheep mineral containing 15 per cent calcium and 10 per cent phosphorus at 25 kg per tonne. The change in ration from mainly straw at housing to mainly cereal at lambing means that calcium will become too low in the last month of pregnancy and may cause problems of the milk fever type. Gradually adding some limestone to the compound, starting three to four weeks before lambing and reaching a maximum of 1 per cent one week before lambing, should avoid any such problems.

Table 25. Compound allowances (kg) to be given with straw to appetite for a lambing percentage of around 180 per cent.

Ewe weight (kg)	Up to 8	Weeks before lambing 6	4	2	Lambing
55	.36	.55	.68	.82	.95
65	.43	.62	.77	.91	1.05
75	.47	.66	.85	1.05	1.18
80	.50	.68	.87	1.09	1.23

As a rough guide the compound allowance on a straw-based diet should be increased by 0.23 kg over the compound that would usually be fed when using hay as the roughage.

Under this straw-feeding system more concentrates are fed than in a more traditional hay-based system but a comparison of costs over a ninety-day housed period favours the straw-feeding system as shown in the following example.

		£
Present straw system:	61 kg concentrates @ £110/t	6.71
	128 kg straw @ £15/t	1.90
		8.61
If hay were fed:	43 kg concentrates @ £107/t	4.60
	128 kg hay @ £40/t	5.12
		£9.72

Ewe hoggs not in lamb and store sheep can be wintered on straw—a ration for animals weighing 25-35 kg would consist of high-quality straw ad lib plus a daily allowance of 0.4 kg per head of a concentrate containing adequate supplementary nutrients. Sheep can be relied upon to pick out the most nutritious part of the straw they are given and this will give it a rather better feeding value.

The Effect of Chemical Treatment of Straw on its Feeding Value for Sheep

There are so far very few practical examples of feeding straw treated with sodium hydroxide or ammonia to ewes. It is known that sheep will readily eat such treated straw and experiments have shown that the intake of straw by sheep is increased by chemical treatment. The problems associated with increased urination may be serious enough when ewes are housed to make sodium hydroxide treatment unsuitable. More information is needed about feeding ammonia-treated straw to ewes before any firm recommendation can be made.

Horses, Goats, Rabbits and Pigs

Straw has traditionally been used for feeding *horses*. Early in the present century a ration for heavy horses given by one authority was as follows:

Ingredient	Idle horses kg	Horses on full work kg
Oat straw	3.7	4.0
Hay	2.7	2.7
Oats	3.7	5.4
Beans or peas	–	1.4
Linseed	–	0.7

In the northern and western parts of the United Kingdom horses were frequently fed a simple ration composed of oat straw fed ad lib and oats fed at rates from 6.4 to 10.8 kg per day according to the nature of the work to be done and the size of the horse.

In wheat-growing areas the chaff was saved especially for feeding to horses, often mixed with sliced mangolds and bean and oat meal. When the chaff ran out, chopped straw would replace it.

Today we are concerned almost exclusively with rations for riding horses, but the same principles apply as for working horses. Recently there have been some interesting experiments reported from West Germany on feeding straw to riding horses. In these experiments 'straw-mix'—a mixture of ground straw, molasses, urea and other ingredients as described in an earlier paragraph—was fed as a complete diet or as a hay supplement and compared with a hay-and-concentrate diet.

Intake of straw appeared to be increased by the straw-mix process but not the digestibility. Horses fed on straw-mix alone appeared to respond less well to high riding demands than when fed concentrates and hay or a combination of concentrates and straw-mix. The recommendation was to restrict the feeding of straw-mix to 5 kg per day per 465 kg of body weight, and to feed cereals for the remaining energy requirement.

Some experiments in Norway compared straw treated with anhydrous ammonia in a stack with untreated straw and straw fed with either urea or soya bean meal to Shetland type ponies. These experiments showed that ammonia treatment improved the energy value of the straw at about 15 per cent. The nitrogen content of the straw was increased by about 50 per cent and the ponies were able to utilise some of this extra crude protein, but their requirements for protein were not met by the ammonia-treated straw.

The use of herbage seed straw in rations for horses has also been studied in Oregon in the United States. This straw is similar in analysis to cereal straw but rather lower in fibre content. It was found that mature mares and geldings readily adapted to rations containing up to 50 per cent of cubed straw and maintained condition. Horses eat cubed straw well and cubing reduces waste.

Ground straw is commonly fed to milking *goats* in France and is being tried in this country. French experience indicates that goats will accept between 1.3 and 1.5 kg dry matter of high-quality straw per 100 kg of liveweight. However, feeding for milk production in goats should follow similar principles to those applying to milking cows and it would be wise to restrict goats in full milk to 0.8 kg per day of high-quality straw, suitably balanced for protein, minerals and vitamins. In France ground straw has been successfully fed to goats.

Rabbits, although not ruminants, have a system of digestion which involves regurgitation and breakdown by enzymes of fibrous food. Cellulose is, indeed, an essential ingredient in rabbit food. Dried lucerne has been a favourite ingredient in the rations of rabbits fed for meat production but experience has shown that cereal straw in a mixture that includes 10 per cent wheat and 10 per cent soya bean cake can replace lucerne. Trials in France showed that satisfactory growth rates and carcase dressing percentages could be obtained from feeds containing up to 30 per cent wheat straw, though feed conversion rate fell when the straw content increased from 20 per cent to 30 per cent. These trials showed that treating the straw with 2 per cent of sodium hydroxide gave no benefit. The digestive system of *pigs* is ill adapted to cope with fibrous food. Pigs bedded on straw may eat some of it and their feed conversion efficiency may be reduced by so doing. It has been noticed that some sows take to chewing their bedding and their milk production and quality may be reduced in this way. Trials have been carried out to see if pigs can make use of straw in which the energy content has been increased by alkali treatment, but the digestibility of the treated straw proved to be very low indeed.

Chapter 5

STRAW AND THE SOIL

IT NEEDS TO BE APPRECIATED that there is much more straw in modern cereal crops than many people realise. Until recently it was widely thought that a tonne per acre or 2½ tonnes per hectare, was a normal yield of straw and this was true of harvested straw when grain production was around 1 tonne per acre or less. Modern baled straw yields probably average not far short of 4 tonnes per hectare and there is a trend towards steadily rising yields, as grain yields increase.

What is not generally realised is that total straw yields are often much higher than baled straw production. ADAS field trials in which winter wheat was cut at harvest time as close as possible to the ground and separated into grain and the remainder gave total yields of straw including all leaf and chaff of between 8½ and 9½ tonnes per hectare for grain yields of 7½ tonnes per hectare, expressed as dry matter.

Thus, even after a crop of around 4 tonnes per hectare of straw has been carted off, there may well remain at least as much straw on the ground. When no straw is removed from the field the quantity that may have to be cultivated or ploughed in is formidable and may often amount to as much as 10 tonnes per hectare with heavy crops.

Physical Nature

Straw is a tough fibrous material in which fibres are partially protected from decay. Unless it is thoroughly broken up and well mixed with moist and well-aerated soil at a sufficiently high temperature to encourage breakdown, a heavy crop of straw incorporated into the soil will make it puffy and impede movement of moisture and nutrients. Straw is a highly absorbent and resilient material with excellent insulation properties and has always made good bedding material for livestock—hence its importance as a base for farmyard manure.

Chemical Properties

Straw contains up to 10 per cent of compounds which readily ferment or decay to form chemicals which can in some circumstances be toxic to plant growth.

The amount of phosphate, potash and calcium varies considerably from sample to sample and table 26 shows a range of values for wheat straw.

Table 26. Phosphate, potash and calcium content of wheat straw as per cent of dry matter.

P_2O_5	K_2O	Ca
0.15 – 0.25	1.0 – 2.25	0.12 – 0.25

Using current fertiliser values of 36p per kg of P_2O_5 and 17p per kg of K_2O, straw with the above analysis would be worth between £2.24 and £4.72 per tonne. Even allowing for a considerable reduction in value owing to the probably lower availability of phosphate and potash in straw ash, it is clear that a 10 tonne per hectare crop of straw has a valuable content of these elements.

A further characteristic of straw which has an important bearing on soil fertility is its high carbon-to-nitrogen ratio. This is of the order of 80 to 1. When bacteria, which have a carbon-to-nitrogen ratio of about 4 to 1 in their bodily structure, feed upon the energy provided by the carbon in the straw they require extra nitrogen and must obtain this either from reserves in the soil or from additional sources which may be provided by the farmer. The effect of the high carbon-to-nitrogen ratio in straw will be considered in the section on field burning, soil incorporation and composting of straw.

The above characteristics of straw have to be taken into

account when considering the effect of various methods of disposal upon soil fertility, cultivations and crop growth.

FIELD BURNING

Field burning has become the main method in England of disposing of several million tonnes of unwanted straw — about half the total straw production. The proportion of straw burned in the field is lower than this in most if not all other European countries. In West Germany, for instance, only 8 per cent is field-burned. However, conditions are different on the Continent.

Methods of Burning

Methods are to some extent dictated by the Code of Practice which has been recommended by the National Farmers Union and usually forms the basis of local bye-laws. This Code is subject to revision from time to time and the latest agreed version is given at Appendix I. It is assumed here that all field burning will be done according to the provisions of the Code (Plate 28). Aside from legislation to control field burning of

28.
Field burning with ploughed fire-break.

29.
Straw spreader fitted to combine.

(Claas)

straw there are also in many farm tenancy agreements clauses requiring tenants to obtain written permission from their landlord or his agent before burning straw left behind the combine.

The commonest method is still to burn the straw without spreading. After the necessary field preparation, the swaths are ignited and, in suitable conditions, the fire will run along the swath and may jump from row to row and perhaps also burn between the swaths. Usually, it is necessary to move the fire by fork from time to time in order to get the full length of the row to burn. A burning tyre towed behind the tractor has been used on some farms to spread the flame and on other farms a hand-held gas flame gun has been used. Although in very dry conditions and with a suitable breeze it is sometimes possible to blacken the whole field by this method, more often the result is to stripe the field with burnt swaths and unburned strips of stubble in between.

Some farmers prefer to spread the straw from the swath before burning. This can be done cheaply by means of a combine-mounted spreader (Plate 29) which deflects the straw as it falls from the straw walkers. These spreaders are driven by a pulley from the combine and require very litle power. They have the disadvantage that they work unevenly in a wind; the straw may even be blown back into the standing corn, making it necessary to combine only down the leeward side of the crop. Some farmers prefer to put a tedder into the field to spread the swath before burning. This is obviously a relatively time-consuming and expensive method but has the advantage that the spreading may be timed to be done when the weather seems right either for an immediate burn or in order to dry the straw for a quick burn.

A few farmers use a straw chopper, either combine-mounted or tractor-operated, to spread straw for field burning. They say that this chopped straw burns evenly and the method has the advantage that, if good burning conditions do not arrive at a suitable time, the field is in any case fit for cultivation.

Surveys have shown that there is an average interval of a week or more between completion of combining and burning the straw. The field has in any case to be prepared for burning, atmospheric conditions have to be suitable, and there may well be adjacent standing crops which it would be unwise to jeopardise.

Burning the stubble after removing the straw in the swath is normally much more difficult to do thoroughly. Sometimes, particularly with barley straw and in very dry conditions with the right breeze, it is possible to achieve a very thorough blackening, but this is the exception rather than the rule.

Even small infestations of green plants will halt the spread of the fire, particularly when stubble burning. The use of desiccant can help to overcome this problem. One method is to apply 1½ pints of paraquat per hectare a few days before intending to burn; another is to apply glyphosate pre-harvest. The latter has the advantage that it should kill rather than desiccate twitch (*Agropyron repens*), but in both cases burning should take place without great delay or some weeds may green up again.

A method of stubble burning which has been developed and tried out on several farms in recent years has been the use of stubble-burning machines (Plate 30). In the United Kingdom such machines use jets of burning oil which spread fire under a steel canopy. They have been tractor mounted and so precautions have to be taken against firing-back towards the tractor. In practice these machines have given variable results. They work best in very dry, clean stubbles where field burning is most

30.
Mechanical stubble burner at work.

(Esso)

successful, and worst in stubbles that are weedy and moist. To get good results in poor conditions they have to work slowly and at greater cost in time and fuel. A firm in the Midlands operated an experimental contract service for a time but this did not expand. In the United States machines were developed to field-burn herbage seed crop residues in Oregon. These relied upon oil to start the fire but then gathered their fire from the straw itself; but again these machines, which were large and costly, did not take over from uncontrolled field burning. It is possible that efficient field-burning machinery may yet be devised but there is nothing available at present for the British farmer.

There have been a few experiments to compare the efficiency of different methods of field burning. At High Mowthorpe Experimental Husbandry Farm, trials carried out in 1980 and repeated in 1981 found that spreading straw from the swath by tedder led to an increase in the amount of stubble blackened in field burning from about 30 per cent in the case of burning down the swath to about 90 per cent when the straw was spread. However, under the conditions of these trials, although the cut straw burned well when spread, the stubble underneath was largely unaffected—whereas both straw and the stubble underneath it were well burned when the swath was burned unspread.

A number of other trials have shown that soil temperature increases little and to only a shallow depth when spread straw is burned. Work at the Weed Research Organisation has shown that the temperature on the surface of the soil during straw burning depends on the amount of straw burned, as shown in Table 27.

Table 27. Temperature on soil surface during straw burning

Amount of straw burned t/ha	Peak-temperature °C	Duration of temperature (sec)	
		above 200°C	above 100°C
2.1	143	0	35
4.2	225	10	60
6.3	270	35	70

The peak temperatures on the soil surface were reached 20-30 seconds after the initial temperature rise and quickly subsided to 40°-50°C on all treatments 2½ minutes later. The temperature reached at 2-3 mm depth was much less than on the soil surface and, with the largest amount of straw, did not exceed 60°C.

The WRO also investigated how long it took to kill blackgrass seeds at different temperatures in an oven. It took one minute at 150°C to kill dry blackgrass seed and five minutes if the seed had taken up moisture. At a temperature of 200°C the corresponding times were 40 seconds (dry) and 50 seconds (moist). From this work it seems that normal straw burning will have little effect upon the viability of seed which is below the surface of the soil and that a good thickness of straw needs to be burned if most blackgrass seed on the surface is to be killed, particularly if the seed has taken up moisture.

In the High Mowthorpe Trials the use of 1½ litres per ha of paraquat as a desiccant gave comparatively little improvement in the burn.

Needless to say, whatever method of burning is employed, the conditions should be right. It will be impossible to obtain a good burn when straw and stubble are damp. It is most unwise to attempt burning when conditions are exceptionally dry or windy. The best conditions are usually when the straw has dried after a dewy morning and when there is a light but steady breeze; and the most thorough burns are usually obtained when burning against the breeze.

The Advantages of Field Burning

The main advantage of field burning is that, in the right conditions, it clears the land quickly and cheaply of an obstruction that would otherwise interfere with work to establish the next crop. When that next crop is to be autumn-sown it is even more important to remove the straw quickly. Surveys carried out in Oxfordshire over a number of years have shown that down-the-swath burning is the commonest method and the cost—mainly in man and tractor hours spent in clearing and cultivating the required strip round the field and in actually carrying out and supervising the burning—is usually less than £2.00 per ha for large fields. If the straw is spread by tedder or if a desiccant is used the cost will of course increase, but field burning as it is usually carried out is a cheap operation.

Field burning often leaves the soil in a friable condition which is suitable for direct drilling. One reason for this is that removing straw and stubble allows the land to dry out more quickly after wetting and this improves surface texture, particularly in a showery late summer and autumn. However, it should be noted that this advantage is reduced if the burn is patchy or if it does not burn the stubble right down.

Field burning may also have an effect on weed seeds. Tests at the Weed Research Organisation have shown that only about half as many blackgrass plants germinate on direct drilled plots after a thorough burn as on unburned plots, although there was little difference on land that was ploughed before drilling. It is known that straw and stubble burning kills some wild oat seed and causes some to germinate more quickly. It is not clear that direct economies can be made in herbicide use as a result of burning but it may be that herbicides are more effective on reduced weed populations that result from straw burning.

It is believed that straw and stubble burning reduce pests and diseases, and it would seem reasonable to expect that the sanitary effects of a good burn would help to keep pests and diseases at bay. Thus, with a disease such as net blotch one might expect a quick spread with winter-barley drilled into a seedbed containing infected straw from the previous barley crop, and that a complete burn of such debris would much reduce the risk of attack. However, it has been difficult to show experimentally that field burning reduces disease. This may be because when conditions favour the spread of disease, quite small amounts of innoculum are sufficient to start the infection. Trials have shown that eyespot, sharp eyespot and take-all were not reduced by burning.

One good result of field burning is that the phosphate and potash content of the burned straw is returned to the soil—though some may be blown away to other areas by wind and convection currents.

It is often claimed that field burning of either stubble or straw and stubble simply leads to better yields. If field burning makes possible the timely sowing of crops that would otherwise be delayed, such a claim may well be justified. The claim may also be justified when the crop is direct drilled and a good even burn has left the land in a better state for direct drilling than would have been possible without burning.

However, the claim that, as a general rule, field burning in itself leads to heavier crops cannot be justified. The belief arises partly because, in official and unofficial comparisons that have been made between sowing after burning straw and/or stubble and sowing without burning, the trials have been done without adding the compensating nitrogen which is needed to overcome temporary denitrification. This point will be taken up again in the section on straw chopping and incorporation in the soil.

In the special case of direct drilling, however, there is evidence that better yields obtained after burning have been at least partly due to the production of toxic chemicals when the soluble constituents in unburned straw break down on or near the soil surface, particularly in wet conditions. When this effect is added to that of the immobilisation of nitrogen caused by the breakdown of the straw, serious reductions in yield due to non-burning may be expected when crops are direct drilled.

Disadvantages of Field Burning

The most important immediate disadvantage of field burning arises from the uncontrollable, indeed capricious, nature of fire. If certain precautions are strictly observed, field burning can be kept under good control but any farmer knows how suddenly the wind can change or how a whirlwind may start and carry fire in an unwanted direction. This has led to the adoption by the National Farmers Union of a Code of Practice (given in full at Appendix I together with some European variations). It is obvious that observing regulations which tend to become tighter inevitably adds to the cost of field burning.

The code is designed to avoid the danger to trees, hedgerows, wildlife, property, or road and rail traffic due to field straw burning which can arise if fires get out of control. It also seeks to minimise air pollution.

Effect of Straw Burning on Soil Organic Matter

Long-term trials on Ministry of Agriculture Experimental Husbandry Farms were designed after the last war to test the effect of different methods of straw disposal on the organic matter and productivity of the soil. Results after a period of some seventeen years are shown in the table 28.

Table 28. Percentage organic matter in soil (0-40cm)

Farm	Year	Farmyard manure applied	Straw ploughed in	Straw burned	Straw removed
Boxworth	1951	2.93	2.96	2.84	2.85
	1968	2.90	2.79	2.62	2.63
Gleadthorpe	1955	2.10	2.20	2.03	1.97
	1969	2.14	2.10	2.03	2.01
High Mowthorpe	1951	3.97	3.93	3.88	3.91
	1968	3.87	3.78	3.60	3.63
Terrington	1951	2.55	2.58	2.43	2.60
	1968	2.38	2.33	2.34	2.36

These results show no clear sign of any greater reduction in soil organic matter after seventeen years of burning as compared with other methods of straw disposal on these four farms. Nor were there reductions in crop yields resulting from burning. Results for the Woburn Farm of the Rothamsted Experimental Station on very light sandy soil which tends to be exceptionally low in organic matter did, however, demonstrate that such soils can benefit in organic matter and yielding capacity from the incorporation of straw residues.

It has to be remembered that roots, stubble and chaff of a cereal crop contain a much greater weight of organic matter than the harvested straw and there is some evidence that the organic matter in the plants' roots produces more humus for a given weight than the organic matter in stubble or straw.

On all but the lightest soils it seems that soil organic matter content and yielding capacity can be maintained for a considerable period of time without returning any of the straw to the land, provided always that good crops with large root systems are grown, usually with the help of considerable amounts of 'artificial' fertiliser. There are those who maintain, with reason, that twenty years is a short time in agriculture and who continue to predict widespread dire consequences to soil fertility as a result of the field burning of straw—but the evidence for this under British conditions on all but a few soils does not exist.

The Effect of Straw Burning on Slugs, Worms and other Soil Fauna

There is some conflicting evidence regarding the effect of burning upon slugs and worms. As might be expected from the comparatively superficial effect on soil temperature of normal straw burning described earlier, little mortality results from burning. However, the incorporation of straw over several years has been shown by Rothamsted to increase the population of deep-burrowing worms when compared with continually burned plots. These worm populations play an important role in promoting good soil texture, particularly when the land is not cultivated, and Rothamsted trials indicate that straw burning, though facilitating crop establishment in direct drilled crops, may in the long term lead to lower crop yields by reducing deep-burrowing earthworm numbers and activity.

There is no clear evidence that straw burning affects slug populations. Straw residues may attract slugs and give the impression of increased numbers but it is notoriously difficult to count slugs in a soil profile. Rothamsted have investigated the effect of different straw disposal systems on other soil fauna, both harmful and beneficial. There is no clear evidence for economically important effects from burning, over a period of years. Surface-inhabiting types such as thrips or aphids are temporarily reduced, but so may be their insect predators.

One effect of burning deserves a mention. Many farmers will have noticed the vigorous crop growth that occurs where a fierce fire of hedge clipping or concentrated crop debris has occurred. Such a fire will heat and sterilise the soil beneath it to a considerable depth. Plant nutrients, in particular nitrogen, which are immobilised in the bodies of soil microbes, will be mineralised and released for use by the growing crop when these microbes are killed. The result is the reverse effect of that produced from nutrient immobilisation when plant residues with a high carbon-to-nitrogen ratio are incorporated.

STRAW CHOPPING AND SOIL INCORPORATION

It is practically impossible, using ordinary ploughs, to plough in long straw, even after it has been spread, soon after combining. It is true that in the Chamberlain system, devised by a farmer in Oxfordshire many years ago, an undersown crop of trefoil could provide the nitrogen to break down straw spread behind the combine given the right conditions and sufficient time— which usually meant delayed ploughing for a spring crop. However, problems associated with undersown crops, including difficulty and expense in establishment and interference with combining in some seasons, have prevented the system from being widely adopted and the only practical alternative to baling and carting off, or burning the straw behind the combine, is to chop and incorporate it in the soil. The straw should be chopped to a length of no more than 3-5 cm.

Before considering what may be termed the conventional methods of straw chopping, mention should be made of the effect on the straw of axial-flow combine harvesters. These recently introduced machines appear to lacerate the straw to a greater degree than conventional combine harvesters, at least under some working conditions. The straw left behind the axial-flow combine tends to be broken and short and may possibly allow certain types of plough to operate, without further chopping.

Methods of Chopping

The cheapest and easiest method for many farmers will be to use a combine-mounted straw chopper (Plates 31 and 32). This consists of rotating or free-swinging knives attached at the rear of the combine so that straw falling from the straw walkers is

31.
Combine-mounted straw chopper.

(Claas)

32.
Combine-mounted straw chopper at work.

(Claas)

chopped and deposited in a wide band. Various widths of chopper are available to suit different combines. They have a power requirement of approximately two to three horse power per tonne chopped but modern combines have sufficient reserves of engine power to operate choppers without loss of output on reasonably level ground. The extra power requirement of the chopper may, however, reduce combine output when travelling uphill or when grain is being transferred to trailers on the move. They will use a little more fuel when operating the chopper. The noise and dust arising from combine-mounted choppers were formerly held against them, but the modern air-conditioned cab overcomes this problem.

Another method is to use a tractor-powered chopper in a separate operation (Plate 33). This has the obvious disadvantage that it is more costly in labour and machinery but the chopper may be used for other work such as potato haulm destruction or grass topping or for chopping up the remains of brassica crops. Tractor-driven choppers have a minimum power requirement of about 10 hp per foot width. A variation of this method is to use a precision-chop forage harvester but this is really only feasible for specific purposes, such as preparing headland strips for ploughing. The power requirement of a precision-chop harvester working in straw is likely to be in excess of 50 hp.

33.
Tractor-operated straw chopper at work.

(John Wilder Engineering)

The Cost of Chopping

The cost of straw chopping will depend on the method employed. For a combine-mounted chopper costing, say, £1700, written off at 15 per cent over ten years, and using a few pints of additional diesel per hectare and assuming that the machine does about 150 hectares per season, the cost of chopping should not exceed about £3.00 per hectare. With a tractor-powered chopper which may be priced at about £3500 at the time of writing, the cost of chopping, involving as it does a separate operation with man and tractor, will certainly be greater, even when the capital cost of the machine can be spread over other operations.

Problems of Incorporation

There has been little interest in the United Kingdom in recent years in straw chopping and incorporation and we lack some essential information on aspects of this problem.

It is not clear how short or uniform a chop is required for different cultivation systems, nor how uniform the distribution should be. It is not clear how important the degree of chopping is for satisfactory decomposition. Nor do we know how thoroughly, and at what depth, the chopped straw should be incorporated in order to favour decomposition. In practice it may be that experience and understanding of the main principles involved will have to determine what the farmer does and there is no easy rule of thumb which can be applied to all soils and conditions. A 5 cm chop length seems a reasonable compromise at the present time and incorporation to a depth of up to 20 cm may often be necessary in order to ensure that the straw has sufficient moisture as well as warmth and air to ensure its breakdown.

There remains a lack of information on the best implements to use to cultivate the land where straw has been chopped. Tandem discs often provide good incorporation of chopped straw but there can be problems of soil penetration and soil compaction using these implements on some soils. Fixed tines and strong spring tines will mix chopped straw and soil but they do not bury it effectively. It may be that a combination of disc and tines will give the best results in many circumstances, possibly used in a tillage train.

Rotary cultivators have some attraction for use where straw has been chopped. The 'Rotadigger' works well in reasonably moist soil conditions and has a good work rate. Rotary cultivators fitted with L-blades would be effective but their work rate is slow. A combination of chisel ploughs and rotary cultivation has given good results on the Continent.

The problem of disposing of the chopped straw is more acute when the land is not to be ploughed. For true 'direct' drilling a layer of chopped straw on the soil surface will present an unacceptable hazard, perhaps preventing coulter penetration and also liable to damage the germinating crop by generating toxins. It may be possible to compromise and employ bridge link systems in which, for instance, disc cultivators operate between the tractor and the drill, but such systems cannot be expected to incorporate the chopped straw sufficiently well to ensure thorough breakdown.

There can be no doubt that in the short run straw chopping

and incorporation in the the soil is the only alternative method of disposal to burning for most of the millions of tonnes of straw that are at present field burned. For land that is to be ploughed the problem may not be acute. For systems that do not include ploughing, cultivation methods, perhaps using combinations of implements, can be evolved to suit different soil types and crop needs. For true direct drilling the only alternative to burning may be to bale and remove the straw.

De-Nitrification Caused by Straw Incorporation and How to Overcome It

A reasonable supply of moisture and warmth is necessary to break down chopped straw in the soil, and for best results the straw should be worked into the soil as soon as possible in order to make the most of suitable weather conditions. Soil-incorporated straw also causes demands upon available soil nitrogen when microbes attack it. In many situations it will be necessary to supply additional nitrogen to overcome temporary soil de-nitrification. The amount and timing of this additional supply of nitrogen cannot be stated precisely for all circumstances. Much depends upon the biological activity of the particular soil and the rate at which nitrogen is being recycled within it. With fields that have been under continuous cereals for some years and which have not had straw incorporated, it might be expected that little readily available nitrogen will be available for the microbes to use, whereas on a field which has recently been ploughed out of a clovery ley it might be expected that recycled nitrogen would be comparatively abundant.

Assuming a total demand of 8 kg of nitrogen per tonne of straw to be broken down, an 8 tonne per ha crop of straw to be incorporated, and a soil capable of supplying about 30 kg of nitrogen, about another 30 kg of nitrogen would be needed to avoid de-nitrification. For winter-sown crops on land which is biologically inactive it may be advisable to apply this extra nitrogen to the field before working in the chopped straw. On other soils it may be best to apply the nitrogen in the spring when the growing crop most needs a ready supply. In any case, all the additional nitrogen is not lost to the system—some at least of it will be released later as biological activity in the soil is encouraged and the recycling of nitrogen through the bodies of the microbes increases. After a few years of straw incorporation, with additional nitrogen, there may be sufficient natural recycling of nitrogen taking place in the soil to obviate the necessity for additional nitrogen dressings when straw is incorporated.

Rothamsted Experimental Station carried out some of the best early fundamental work on the so-called 'nitrogen factor' in the breakdown of straws, but we have up till now put little emphasis on the importance of ensuring that there is plenty of available nitrogen when straw is incorporated in the soil. During early years of the long-term disposal trials at the Ministry's Experimental Husbandry Farms referred to earlier in this section, extra nitrogen was added to the straw-incorporated plots. It was found that these plots gave increased yields and it was considered that the extra nitrogen received gave them an unfair advantage and this extra nitrogen dosage was stopped. In more recent straw disposal trials by EHFs no additional nitrogen was given to the straw-incorporated plots and it should have come as no surprise that straw-burned plots gave better yields. In Great Britain probably less than 1 per cent of cereal straw is now chopped and incorporated in the soil whereas in West Germany it is estimated that 25 per cent of straw is so treated and in France the latest available estimate is 22 per cent chopped and incorporated. In both countries the 'nitrogen factor' is well understood and farmers are advised accordingly.

STRAW FOR LITTER AND THE PRODUCTION OF MANURE

Straw has been used as bedding for livestock for many centuries, but its use for this purpose has been viewed more critically by United Kingdom farmers in recent decades.

There is no doubt that housed animals look well and contented when bedded on clean dry straw (Plate 34). They tend to keep warmer in cold weather when there is plenty of straw and the fermenting yard manure itself generates heat. One has the impression that animals in these conditions may fatten more economically and there is experimental evidence, for instance, that pigs in low environmental temperatures housed on concrete slabs need more food for a given rate of live weight gain than do pigs on straw bedding. On the other hand it has been shown that lactating sows housed on straw, though

34.
Pigs on straw in a Lincolnshire yard, 1955.

(Author)

comfortable, chewed and ate too much straw so that their litters suffered from a reduced milk supply. For racehorses there seems nothing to beat plenty of clean dry straw for bedding.

As well as providing a comfortable bed for stock, straw has the advantage that it absorbs the dung and urine. The resulting manure can be handled and moved with comparatively simple equipment, and it has a value as a soil conditioner and fertiliser. Indeed, for centuries, farmyard manure was greatly valued as a fertiliser and livestock were often kept as much for the provision of manure as for their own profitability. The handling of straw bedding and of the resultant manure was laborious and still presents problems, even with modern machinery.

Much effort has been put into the development of slurry-handling systems, so that straw bedding can be eliminated and the disposal of dung and urine can be completely mechanised. This and the enormous increase in the use of 'artificial' fertilisers has led to the whole practice of using straw for livestock bedding being questioned. The following paragraphs look at some of the facts of the case in relation to different classes of stock.

Cattle

Cattle in covered yards weighing about 450 kg need about 5 kg of straw per day per head and can be given up to about 10 kg. This means a consumption of between one and two tonnes per head for a 200-day yarding period. Such cattle will produce about 7 tonnes of farmyard manure per head while in the yard. An average analysis of yard manure from these cattle might be as shown in table 29.

Table 29. Average analysis of cattle manure per tonne.

Nitrogen (N)	6.0 kg
Phosphate (P_2O_5)	4.0 kg
Potash (K_2O)	10.0 kg

However, experiments have shown that the availability of these nutrients and particularly of the nitrogen is much lower than that in 'artificial' fertilisers which can be applied to the crop when they are needed. At present prices per kg the elements in the above table would give the manure a value of about £5.00 per tonne, but a more realistic value is no higher than, perhaps, £2.50 per tonne. Thus it may be calculated that one or two tonnes of straw bedding under yarded cattle may be transformed into around 7 tonnes of manure worth about £17.50—a very bulky, low-value product. It may be claimed that farmyard manure also supplies minor elements and valuable organic matter. However, as in the case of incorporated straw in the soil, discussed earlier, it has been impossible to prove the economic value of these aspects of manure in modern farm practice. Potatoes have responded comparatively well to applications of farmyard manure, probably because of its potash content, but cereals show only a small return from it. In view of the increasing specialisation of cereal production, it is hardly surprising that cattle yard manure has lost popularity as an agent in soil fertility over large areas of the country. This unpopularity has been increased by the comparatively poor return that can be obtained from beef cattle and the high capital investment required by beef enterprises.

On mixed farms, particularly those growing spring-sown root and vegetable crops which provide a better opportunity for the field spreading of manure, the use of straw in the production of yard manure may still have advantages.

So far as dairy cattle are concerned the number of herds has approximately halved in the past ten years, while the proportion kept in cubicles has increased from about a tenth to about a half. Various types of bedding have been tried in cubicles and chopped straw is now widely favoured. It has been found that cows can be kept comfortable in cubicles with small amounts of chopped straw—it has been possible to halve the allowance from about 1½ kg per cow per day of long straw (Plate 35) to ¾ of a kg per cow per day with chopped straw. This straw can be coarsely chopped and stored in a convenient building to be spread at intervals of a few days by hand from a trolley; or it can be chopped from the bale by a small machine and blown directly into the cubicle. It is claimed that the labour requirement for bedding with chopped straw—at 30 man minutes per cubicle for a 180-day winter—is only half that for bedding with long straw from bales.

It seems unlikely that there will be any large increase in the

35.
About half as much straw is required for cow cubicles if it is chopped.

use of straw for bedding cattle. There would need to be a great increase in the cost of 'artificial' fertiliser—in particular nitrogen —before yard manure became attractive again for its fertiliser value.

In the event of beef production becoming more profitable, it is worth noting that 250,000 more cattle would be needed in the counties of Norfolk, Suffolk and Essex alone to bring the ratio of cattle numbers to cereal acres up to where it was in 1955. These extra cattle could be expected to absorb up to 200,000 tonnes of straw as bedding.

Pigs

Many of the points made in connection with straw bedding for cattle also apply to pigs. The amount of straw required per animal needs to be scaled down, but the quality of the manure produced is not dissimilar, being rather higher on average in phosphate and rather lower in potash content.

There has been a marked swing in recent decades to keeping pigs on concrete, but, in certain districts, particularly where the farmyard manure can be advantageously used for root and vegetable crops, straw bedding has many advantages for pigs.

For farrowing sows and for their litters, a small amount of coarsely ground straw for bedding has been found suitable. Straw put through a hammer mill with a coarse sieve has proved satisfactory.

One factor which may influence the use of straw for pigs is the objectionable odour of stored pig slurry when it is moved and spread. Public protests against the spreading of pig slurry may force farmers to reconsider the use of straw bedding for their fattening units.

Poultry

Changes in farming practice have led to an increase in the demand for straw for bedding for one class of stock—poultry. Although in the United Kingdom very few layers are kept on litter, the vast majority of fattening poultry (broilers and turkeys) are housed on litter. Wood shavings were for some time the favourite basis for this, but straw is becoming increasingly popular when broilers are kept in straw-producing areas.

It is estimated that about a quarter of a tonne of straw is required per thousand broilers. Experience is showing that a coarsely milled (to a length of about 5 cm) rather than chopped straw is most suitable for this purpose. Such straw has great absorbency and does not compact badly. There are contract grinding services available which will grind required quantities and blow the litter direct into broiler houses for subsequent spreading to the desired depth. The straw can be treated in the process with a suitable fungicide to control the growth of moulds, such as *Aspergillus fumigatus*. Small portable grinding machines are also available for grinding conventional bales in broiler houses and these have given good results.

The cost of grinding straw for broiler litter is estimated at the time of writing to be about £15.00 per tonne. Some broiler producers on cereal-growing farms have claimed big savings in the cost of litter, since the price of delivered wood shavings increased to more than £50.00 per tonne, particularly as only about half as much straw, by weight, is required as compared with wood shavings.

It should be emphasised, however, that even if all the broilers and turkeys in the United Kingdom changed to straw litter, the total quantity of straw for this purpose would amount to only about 100,000 tonnes per annum.

The fertiliser value of broiler litter is much higher than that of cattle manure as shown in table 30.

Table 30. Average analysis of broiler litter per tonne

Nitrogen (N)	18 kg
Phosphate (P_2O_5)	23 kg
Potash (K_2O)	14 kg

As in the case of cattle manure, the availability of the above nutrients may be only about half that of the N P and K in 'artificial' fertilisers, so that the broiler litter would be valued at about approximately £7.00 per tonne.

COMPOSTING

The use of straw and other organic residues to make compost has been understood for a very long time. The process is particularly well known to gardeners who use it to convert leaves and other plant waste material into compost which improves soil texture and adds fertility. Considerable hand labour is usually expended in making and moving the compost heap, and gardeners know that a judicious mixture of mainly fibrous material with other more nitrogen-rich material is essential to success.

From time to time it has been suggested that the process might well be carried out on a much larger scale on farms, using surplus straw as the basis for the compost. The process has been investigated scientifically at many laboratories and field stations and certain principles have been established for successful composting. Sufficient nitrogen must be available to enable the bacteria to break down the organic matter. There must not be excessive acidity; there must be good aeration of the mass, and both excessive wetness or dryness inhibit the necessary bacterial activity. Heat in the compost heap also plays a part and temperatures between 30° and 40°C appear to be best.

Many experiments have been made on composting straw and both world wars stimulated investigations at Rothamsted and elsewhere into the making of 'synthetic manure' from surplus straw. There has been some renewed interest recently in the possibility of mixing pig and cattle slurry and poultry manure— all comparatively rich in nitrogen—with some of the straw which would otherwise be burned. Birmingham University has carried out extensive practical trials into possible techniques of large-scale compost making. Unfortunately there have been serious problems, so far insuperable, in the mechanical handling of very large quantities of straw and ensuring adequate mixing of the slurry, while maintaining correct temperature, oxygen supply and moisture control. What is possible on a small scale, using a hand fork in the garden, has proved impossible on a large scale.

All experimental work on compost shows that there are large losses of nitrogen in the process. There would appear, indeed, to be strong arguments in favour of applying chopped straw and nitrogen to the land and allowing the breakdown of the organic matter to take place there at a season and in conditions which favour the process of breakdown, assisted, if necessary, by cultivations. Composting straw for arable crops is now virtually unknown in this country and there seems no prospect of it becoming a practical system.

Mushroom Compost

Mushroom growers, however, have perfected techniques for composting straw and they annually use about 150,000 tonnes of straw in the United Kingdom for this purpose. Wheat straw is preferred and straw from horse stables is considered a good base for mushroom compost, though pig and cattle manure are also used. Fresh straw can be used to make so-called 'synthetic' compost with the help of nitrogen-rich additions. Different growers have their own recipes for mushroom compost but the essential features of the process are proper mixing of the ingredients, moisture control and aeration. Large machines have been developed which work down the long heaps of compost, chopping, mixing and turning it as they go (Plate 36). It is obvious that this process is much too expensive for the production of a substitute for farmyard manure for application to arable land, although essential for supplying an ideal medium for the growth of mushroom mycelium. Spent mushroom compost is a mixture of compost and the 'casing' which usually consists of a mixture of peat and chalk or ground limestone and is the layer, placed above the compost, in which the mushrooms spawn. An average analysis of fresh, undried, spent compost is as shown in table 31.

Table 31. Analysis of spent mushroom compost in percentages of fresh material

Moisture	N	P_2O_5	K_2O	Ash-free dry matter
64	0.6	0.5	0.9	13

Spent mushroom composts are quite similar to farmyard manure in analysis and in the results they give. Materials used in disease and pest control may occasionally be present in sufficient quantity to be harmful to crops. BHC can taint root crops and DDT is toxic to cucumbers and related crops. However, these insecticides are now seldom used in mushroom production. Spent composts also contain relatively large amounts of soluble salts which could be harmful when applied to some glasshouse soils.

36.
Composting straw for mushrooms.

Straw Bales for Glasshouse Crops

Soon after the last war a horticultural sundriesman in the Lea Valley began selling to commercial growers straw bales impregnated with calcium cyanamide which supplied the necessary nitrogen for the breakdown of straw. The treated bales did not form a true compost but they provided an excellent rooting medium for certain crops. In the process of fermentation a useful amount of heat was produced. In addition it has been found that, in the breakdown of the straw, the concentration of carbon dioxide in the glasshouse atmosphere is increased threefold. The bales require no cultivation and harbour little or no disease; at the end of the season only a small amount of well-rotted straw is left to be worked into the soil.

Several types of crop were tried out on this system but cucumbers proved to be particularly well suited to it and a large proportion of the United Kingdom cucumber crop is grown on straw bales (Plate 37). The technique of using straw bears some resemblance to composting. The bales have first to be thoroughly wetted. Then suitable mixtures of nitrogen and other fertilisers are damped into the bales. There is some discretion as to the correct quantities of the fertilisers, particularly nitrogen, that need to be added. About 7 kg per tonne of nitrogen seems to be about right—this is very close to the quantity which Rothamsted research work showed to be necessary to provide bacteria with sufficient nitrogen to fully break down straw. As with mushroom composts, the temperature of the bales goes up sharply as fermentation proceeds and planting should be delayed until several days after peak heat has been reached, when the temperature has reached about 38°C and is falling. A small quantity of coarse peat is usually placed on top of the bale and the crop is planted in this peat. Once planted the crop will need regular watering, or trickle irrigation. It has been found that weathered and slightly damp bales are suitable for this system

37.
Most cucumbers in the United Kingdom are grown on straw bales.
(Crown copyright)

38.
Strawberry strawing machine working in Worcestershire.

and they should be dense and firmly tied. It is estimated that about 16,000 tonnes of straw are used annually in this way, mainly for cucumbers, and wheat straw is preferred.

Straw for Strawberries
Another traditional horticultural use for straw is for putting beneath the developing fruit of strawberries to keep them free from soil contamination. Barley straw is the most suitable as it is pliable and easily tucked around the plants. Machines have been developed which lay out the straw between the strawberry rows so that it can be quickly tucked under the plants by hand labour (Plate 38). The total quantities of straw used for strawberries is not very large and probably amounts to no more than 10,000 tonnes annually.

Dangers of Herbicide Residues
There have been a few disastrous incidents in which horticultural crops have been ruined when they came into contact with straw containing certain herbicide residues. There are two persistent herbicides that must be avoided:

- 2, 3, 6 – TBA   - 3, 6 – Dichloropicolinic Acid.

39.
Straw-planting machine developed in the United Kingdom.
(H.J. Mason)

These two chemicals are usually mixed with dicamba, mecoprop or MCPA and are sold by several firms under different names.

The grower proposing to use straw for horticulture should make sure that it has not been treated with one of these persistent chemicals. Even farmyard manure and spent mushroom compost made from straw sprayed with these artificial chemicals has been known to ruin horticultural crops.

There is also a danger from the straw of cereal crops which have been sprayed with Glyphosate just before harvest in order to kill couch grass (*Agropyron repens*). The danger applies to glasshouse crops, strawberries and cane fruits and top fruit when straw is used as mulch, and Glyphosate-affected straw may also possibly damage mushrooms.

Planting Straw to Prevent Wind Erosion

Nothing is more frustrating to farmers on 'blow-away' soils than to see newly established crops blown out of the soil by wind erosion. Some soils are particularly bad and it has been known for crops to need redrilling more than once. Machines have been developed which will plant long straw in rows which check the surface-hugging winds that take out young seedlings

(Plate 39). These machines press the straw into peat soils which are particularly subject to blowing. The straw is planted between the rows of the vulnerable crop and provides immediate protection while not competing for plant nutrients and remaining unaffected by herbicides (Plate 40). Disadvantages are that the straw can interfere with tractor hoeing and it has been noticed that birds are sometimes attracted to the straw and then to the crop seedlings. It has been calculated that about 1 tonne per ha of straw is needed for this control of wind erosion and that three men would take about 2½ hours to plant 1 ha, using a machine.

40.
Planted rows of straw prevent wind erosion on fen peat soil in eastern England.

Chapter 6

SUMMARY: THE FUTURE FOR STRAW INCLUDING OUTLETS OFF THE FARM

IN THE INTRODUCTORY chapter the reasons for the present problem of surplus straw disposal—increased cereal production and changes in farm practice—were described. Before summarising possible solutions to the problem, it is worth asking if the trends that have led to the surplus may be reversed and if the problem will diminish without the need for special action. The following assessment, covering the next five to ten years, involves speculation and the conclusions must to some extent be tentative.

Will Straw Production Increase?
The present trend of cereal production in the United Kingdom is still upwards. It seems unlikely that there will be any reduction in the next few years and world population trends point to large increases in demand for cereals in the coming decades.

Most growers and plant breeders agree that the trend towards shorter-strawed varieties and lower straw-to-grain ratios has now slackened and that there will probably be little further reduction in this ratio in the foreseeable future.

It therefore seems unlikely that straw production, which has already reached about 13 million tonnes per annum in the United Kingdom, will diminish; it is more likely to increase.

Will Cereal Harvesting Methods Change?
The combine harvester is now used to harvest virtually all our cereals. A return to whole-crop harvesting, using a form of forage harvester, is still a possibility and practical trials are being carried out. However, there seems no question that most

United Kingdom cereal crops will continue to be combine harvested for at least the next ten years. This means that straw will continue to be dropped behind the combine and that pick-up baling will continue to be the chief method of harvesting straw.

Will There Be a Return to Mixed Farming?

As shown in the introduction, there has been a marked fall in cattle numbers in Eastern England over the past twenty-five years, while the cereal area has considerably increased. To reverse this trend in the three counties of Norfolk, Suffolk and Essex alone, so as to bring the ratio of cattle numbers to cereal area back to where it was in 1955, would call for an increase in the cattle population of approximately 250,000 head. This would require a very large injection of capital. There will need to be a marked improvement in the profitability of beef production before any such swing back to mixed farming in East Anglia can be expected. Full use of arable by-products, including straw, might assist in attaining profitability; but, even if straw were used plentifully for feeding and bedding, the increased cattle numbers would utilise only a fraction of the surplus straw in that area.

It is possible that more straw may be used for some pig herds, but others are giving up straw bedding and any large increase in the use of straw for littering pigs seems unlikely. More straw is being used as litter for poultry but the increased consumption of straw for this purpose will probably not exceed 100,000 tonnes per annum. It is impossible to imagine that working farm horses, once important users of straw, will ever return in significant numbers.

The importance of mixed farming in mainly arable areas was traditionally related to the value of farmyard manure. The value of FYM has probably never been rated so low in arable farming districts as it is today. There is now almost complete reliance on inorganic fertilisers over many parts of the country. It may be that evidence will emerge to support the dire warning of organic farming enthusiasts that the inherent fertility and healthful reserves of the soil are being drained by continual reliance upon 'chemical' fertilisers. For the moment, however, there is no such conclusive evidence and farmers must be influenced by the comparative cheapness of inorganic fertilisers and the accuracy and ease of their use. Their manufacture depends greatly upon supplies of relatively cheap oil and gas, and eventually a shortage of these fuels and a steep increase in their price may force a reappraisal of the value of FYM, and thus encourage a return to mixed farming in the arable east. However, this seems unlikely to happen within the next five to ten years.

In the Midlands and West of England, mixed farming is still important and it may be that the march to monoculture will be halted in these rather moister western areas. It is already noticeable that there is increased interest in straw utilisation for stock in the existing mixed farming areas. Practices like whole-crop harvesting, mixing grass with silage and chaff-saving may find more immediate application in existing mixed farming areas away from the arable East and there may be a strengthening of mixed farming in these areas.

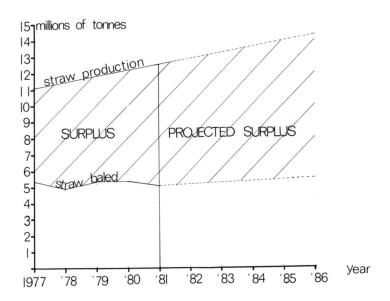

Fig. 10. Estimated straw production and surplus 1977-86 (assuming continuation of present trends).

The most likely development of the straw surplus over the coming 5 years is shown in figure 10. The surplus will increase to 10 million tonnes in England and Wales in 1987 unless much more straw is baled for use.

Can feasible and economic methods of utilising the surplus be introduced? The following paragraphs touch upon the future of field burning and then summarise prospects for increased farm use of straw.

On-Farm Uses for Straw

Will Field Burning Continue to be the Main Method of Surplus Straw Disposal?

With the growth in cereal production, burning has become an important method of disposing of surplus straw. In order to meet the problems this can cause, the National Farmers Union introduced their code of practice which has recently been strengthened. In addition, many local authorities have introduced by-laws based on the enforcible parts of the code.

The same trend in cereal growing on the Continent of Europe and in parts of North America has led to similar problems of straw disposal; legislation relating to field burning has been introduced in most European countries and in several parts of the United States.

In the United Kingdom, in spite of much research into other uses for surplus straw, it seems unlikely that for the forseable future there will be any major alternative to burning as the most cost-effective means of disposing of surplus straw quickly and efficiently.

The emphasis here is to encourage properly controlled burning to ensure that it is done with as little risk as possible and to minimise disturbance to the general public.

Soil Incorporation

If the field burning of straw becomes more restricted and expensive, by far the biggest change in methods of disposal within the next five to ten years is likely to be in the direction of chopping and soil incorporation. If suitable methods of chopping, cultivation and manuring can be worked out, some millions of tonnes of straw may be annually incorporated in the soil within the next five to ten years. Chopping and soil incorporation are unsuitable in direct drilling systems. If burning becomes impossible, straw on land to be direct drilled would have to be removed by baling or other means.

Straw for Fuel in Agriculture and Horticulture

In the past five years there have been improvements in three aspects of straw use as a fuel. These are in controlled automatic stoking, furnace design and the densification of straw fuels.

The drawbacks of straw as a fuel have not been completely overcome but they have certainly been reduced. During recent years the price of coal and oil has risen almost without interruption. The cost of processing straw for convenient stoking and efficient combustion remains high but there are signs that the material is becoming competitive as a fuel for purposes such as glasshouse heating, grain drying and domestic hot water supply, when the raw material can be supplied at a low price. If field burning becomes more expensive, the attraction of using straw as a fuel may increase. There is a prospect that 500,000 tonnes of straw could be used as fuel in agriculture and horticulture within the next decade.

Straw for Feed

It was at one time thought that 500,000 tonnes of sodium hydroxide treated straw could be substituted for barley in compound cattle feeds in this country. In fact the present market (1981-2) is for about one-third of that figure. If the price of barley were to increase sharply the use of alkali-treated straw could increase.

Ammonia treatment of straw to produce a medium-grade hay substitute on the farm may become more widespread but this form of chemical treatment has yet to prove itself on a wide scale. If economical means to avoid waste of ammonia can be worked out and costs thereby reduced, there is a chance that a few hundred thousand tonnes of straw could be treated annually in this way.

The use of straw to absorb effluent from direct cut high-quality silage is at the early farm trial stage. Its success will depend upon a reversal of the widely advocated practice of wilting before ensiling and it is far too early to predict any such widespread reversal. However, if there were a change to direct-cut-silage, there could be a large demand for straw to absorb effluent, assuming that farmers obtain good results from feeding the soaked straw.

Other methods of feeding straw which are claimed to be superior, such as mixing with urea/molasses supplements or feeding in a special 'straw mix' have yet to prove that they are economically justified on a wide scale. They can undoubtedly improve straw intakes by cattle and may tend to increase overall straw consumption by replacing hay.

Attention to the differences that appear to exist in the feeding quality of the straw from different varieties of cereals may enable nutritionally more valuable straw to be selected and this could lead to a greater use of straw for feeding.

OFF-FARM USES FOR STRAW

There has always been some sale of straw for off-farm use. On cereal-growing farms near the big cities large quantities of long straw were formerly trussed and despatched to the cities for use in horse stables or as a packing material or for palliasse making or similar trades. There is still a trade of up to 300,000 tonnes per annum in straw for riding horse stables and mushroom composting with much smaller quantities going for making board, archery targets, rope or for other small crafts.

A few large estates own thrashing machines with reed-combing attachments, and other farms hire this equipment. Some large farms have installed machinery to chemically treat straw and pellet it for sale as a feeding stuff. Cereal-growing farmers may need to consider seriously all possible opportunities to sell straw for use off farms and be prepared if necessary to process straw to some extent to prepare it for market. This might be done in co-operatively run plants, as happens with other agricultural products, and there could be national or EEC grants available to assist such enterprises.

The final section looks at some of the possible outlets for straw off the farm. Some could take hundreds of thousands of tonnes; others only small quantities. But the time may have come when farmers and the agricultural industry in general should promote economic off-farm outlets for straw.

Making Board

Straw is potentially much more valuable as a source of fibre than it is as fuel. The fibre can be used in many ways of which the following are examples.

'Stramit' Board has been made in East Anglia for over thirty years (shown in Plate 41). In this process bales of clean dry straw are gravity fed into a hopper in which the level of the straw is maintained by photo-electric cells which activate the delivery mechanism. From the bottom of the hopper mechanical fingers

41.
Stramit board-making machines.

(Stramit International)

42.
'Strawbox' straw factory at Sittingbourne, Kent

(Straw Box Systems Ltd.)

pull out the straw which is then rammed between the top and bottom beds of a slab-forming mechanism, impacting it against the straw already between the beds. The straw is forced through these beds, which are heated to around 220⁰C, as the slab progresses, by thermostatically controlled electrical elements. It is then set permanently into the compressed state and lined with paper. The waxes, lignins and hemicelluloses which occur naturally in the straw act as binding agents at the temperature and pressure reached in the process and no added binder is required. The board is typically 50 mm thick and 1200 mm wide and is cut into panel lengths of between 2 and 4 m. The board has excellent thermal and sound-insulating properties and is resistant to fire. It is made in many different countries. The 'Stramit' board-making process is a comparatively simple one and the product currently sells at around £210 per tonne—a much higher price than compacted straw could command as a fuel. However, the market is comparatively limited and there seems no possibility that it could exceed 30,000 tonnes per annum in the United Kingdom.

A new process for making a board known as 'strawbox' is being pioneered in Kent (Plate 42). In this process coarsely chopped straw is mixed with a binder and compressed into board of 4 mm thickness which is then die-cut into shapes for making into items such as fruit boxes. This is an entirely new process which still has to show that it can compete with the traditional sources of box wood. If it succeeds there should be opportunities to put up small straw box factories, using perhaps 5000 tonnes of straw each per annum, at convenient sites in straw-producing areas.

Excellent particle board of varying densities can be made from chaffed or ground straw and a suitable binder. Such board has not yet been made commercially in this country, and straw particle board will always have to compete with similar board made from waste wood from the timber industry—which means that profit margins on the process can never be high. However, the process is well understood and if supplies of good-quality straw can be assured at low prices there seems no reason why commercial production should not be attempted.

Paper
About 350,000 tonnes of straw were annually used for making paper in the United Kingdom at the end of the last war, but now none is used here for that purpose. Yet there are many examples of the successful use of straw for paper making on the continent of Europe and there seems to be no good reason why a very large tonnage should not again be made into paper in this country.

The fibre in straw resembles that in hard woods and is particularly suited to the making of such grades as fine writing paper or the corrugating medium used in cardboard boxes. It is not suitable for newsprint for which pulp derived from soft woods is normally used.

The process of pulping straw for paper manufacture is essentially similar to that of treating it with alkali to improve its value as cattle food. The straw is chopped, 'cooked' with a suitable chemical to break down the lignin bonds, ground further and then delivered as a slurry to the paper-making machine. For the manufacture of the coarse brown paper known as corrugating medium only a comparatively small amount of grinding and mild chemical treatment are required and the yield of pulp is high—between 65 and 80 per cent of the straw. For high-grade paper, more grinding and chemical

treatment, including bleaching, are required and the yield drops
to between 35 and 40 per cent of the straw. Semi-chemical pulp
for coarse paper is currently valued at around £200 and
bleached pulp at around £300 per tonne.

Examples of the use of straw for making paper can be studied
in Denmark and Eastern Europe and in several Mediterranean
countries. As an example, a factory at Zaragoza in northern
Spain uses 100,000 tonnes of straw per annum for this purpose,
buying in straw mainly through contractors who purchase it in
the swath and then bale and stack it locally for later delivery on
a sliding scale of prices (Plate 43). The value of straw at factory
is low, in the region of £20.00 per tonne (1981). This means
that the farmer can expect no more than £5.00 per tonne in the
swath.

43.
Buffer store of straw at Zaragoza paper factory.

(Author)

Fuel

Ordinary baled straw has the disadvantage that is very bulky for
economical transport and storage and this drawback will
restrict its use off the farm. However, there are some situations
off the farm in which baled straw may be competitive with coal,
usually when large amounts of heat are required at sites

adjacent to abundant straw supplies. Examples are for glasshouse heating, malt or hop drying or even communal hot water supplies to villages or towns situated in cereal-growing areas. There are indications that large straw burning boilers—supplying 1,000 MJ or more per hour—can compete with mineral hydrocarbon-fuelled boilers in such situations, with fully auto- mated stoking. For economic operation, such heating units must be assured of adequte supplies of dry straw at a delivered price averaging no more than £20.00 per tonne (1982). This may well limit the economic range of straw to about twenty-five miles. During the next decade a number of such outlets may materialise and they could use a substantial quantity of straw— perhaps several hundred thousand tonnes. The technology of collecting and using straw as a fuel is being developed and the economies of the various systems may well improve within the next few years.

If the problem of low density could be economically overcome by briquette or pellet production to form a clean fuel which could be automatically stoked, there would be a considerable potential market for straw as a fuel. However, the value per tonne of this fuel will always have to be related to that of coal and oil fuels which have, respectively, about twice and about three times the energy value of straw. A considerable effort is being made in several European countries to develop more economic methods of densifying straw. With improved efficien- cies at every stage—field collection, transport, storage, chopping, conveying and cubing—it may be possible to produce a straw- based fuel that can compete with other fuels on markets distant from the farm. Already in Denmark a number of unprofitable grass-drying plants have turned over to the production of straw pellets, and in France some co-operative lucerne-drying plants have been pelleting straw for fuel in the non-growing season.

If a number of maltings turn to the use of straw as fuel, some tens of thousands of tonnes would be needed for this purpose.

Horticultural Purposes

About half the heated glasshouse area of England and Wales is situated in the eastern part of the country from Humberside to Kent and is therefore likely to be close to areas of surplus straw production. A number of growers who have close links with adjacent farmers have already experimented with straw fuel-heating systems. The early trials were made with some of the hardier crops such as azaleas or bedding plants for which the maintenance of steady high temperature is not critical. But one or two tomato growers have recently gone over to straw fuel-heating systems. *Mushroom houses* sited in cereal growing areas have also been successfully heated by using straw as fuel, and the procurement of straw for this purpose can be organised alongside that of materials needed for composting. Experiments are also being made into the use of the spent compost as fuel, but its high moisture content has proved an obstacle. Another use for straw as fuel in the horticultural industry is in the heating of packing houses which are often situated on or near cereal-growing farms.

It is impossible to make any precise estimate of the likely uptake of straw as a fuel for horticultural purposes. Growers who can ensure reliable supplies of dry straw at a low price can make economies in fuel costs, particularly when compared with oil, but at considerable loss in convenience. If a quarter of the 700 hectares or so of heated glass situated in the main cereal-growing areas were to change to straw as a fuel, they would require perhaps 250,000 tonnes of straw per annum.

Intensive Livestock .
Straw-burning boilers have been used in Denmark and East Anglia for heating *pig houses*. There are no known examples of *broiler houses* being heated by straw but some interest has been expressed in the possibilities for so doing on farms which also produce surplus straw. There seems no reason why straw should not be successfully used as a fuel for such intensive livestock units. With modern insulated houses the heat requirement is comparatively small but there may be possibilities for a few thousand tonnes of straw to be used for heating such houses.

Another possibility which is worth investigating is the use of straw to heat *commercial fish production* units in which water temperature plays a significant part in determining profitability.

In the same context may be mentioned the provision of hot water for dairies. There are examples of straw-burning boilers being used to provide hot water for this purpose but it can be economic only when the boiler is used to supply hot water for other requirements as well.

District Heating

The Svendborg experiment has been described. Clearly there is limited scope for making economies in fuel costs by using straw when the supply of that straw has to be obtained from a large area. However, experience in this country and abroad has shown that it is possible to organise such supplies, in amounts up to some tens of thousands of tonnes per annum, at prices below £20.00 per tonne delivered to site. At these prices and with efficient boilers it may be possible for straw to be competitive with coal as a source of energy, using the most modern and efficient straw-burning boilers, perhaps in conjunction with municipal solid waste as a complementary fuel. If such installations prove successful, there could ultimately be considerable possiblities for a large uptake—running perhaps to a few hundred thousand tonnes per annum—of straw for fuel in areas such as East Anglia.

To sum up, it has to be said that straw as a fuel has serious limitations, but there appear to be some situations in which it can compete commercially with coal and with oil. Some of the possibilities are outlined above and it seems that up to one million tonnes (supplying some 15 TkJ of energy) of the estimated 6-7 million tonnes at present burned or wasted in the field could find a use as fuel within the foreseeable future. The inducement to use more straw as a fuel will obviously be greater if there are further increases in the price of fossil fuels. If, on the other hand, the price of straw were driven up by heavy demand, as might occur locally, it would become less competitive as a fuel.

Other Uses for Straw Fibre

There are many other uses for straw fibre. Straw rope is still made in the United Kingdom on a small scale for packing purposes. There is a small industry at Guildford making high-quality archery targets. Bee skeps and baskets are still made commercially in Somerset.

There are some further possibilities for large-scale use of straw fibre. It has been shown that straw fibre can substitute for asbestos fibre in cement products and there is a potentially large market for it for this purpose. A concrete block maker in Essex has already pioneered the production of 'strawcrete' blocks. In Oregon it has been shown that straw fibre makes an excellent substitute for peat for some horticultural purposes and for the production of worms. For many of these possible outlets it sometimes seems that the greatest need is for an effective development and marketing organisation.

Chemicals

There is an almost infinite variety of chemicals that can be produced from straw. It has been known for half a century that alcohol-like substances which can be used, for instance, in internal combustion engines, can be made from it. Unfortunately, the fermentable material in straw is locked up in its lignified structure and it requires an extra, expensive, stage of preparation before it can be transformed, like sugar cane or starchy waste material, into useful liquid fuel. At the present time there seems little likelihood that straw can economically be used in the manufacture of chemicals.

The potential uses for straw off the farm in the foreseeable future may be summed up as follows:

- There are some large markets for straw for use as a fuel in direct combustion within sight.
- There are clear possibilities for greater use of straw in board-making.
- Large quantities could be used for paper-making if decisions were taken by the paper-making industry to make the necessary investment.
- There are a number of other uses for the fibre in straw which could probably be developed.

None of these uses, however, hold out the possibility of a bonanza to the farmer. At the time of writing it seems that all actual or potential large users of straw for processing offer a price, delivered to the factory or furnace, of around £20.00 per tonne averaged over the year. Translated to a price in the swath, this will be no better than about £5.00 per tonne, or perhaps £20.00 per hectare with average yields. For such a price to hold an attraction, the farmer must be assured that the straw will be removed promptly from the land after the passage of the combine.

To sum up the outlook for straw disposal in the next decade, the foregoing possibilities are shown in diagrammatic form in figure 11.

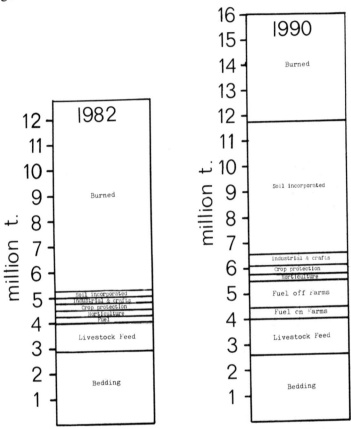

Fig. 11. *Possible changes in straw production and utilisation in England and Wales, 1982-90 (smaller fractions not strictly to scale).*

Figure 11 is based upon assumptions that have already been discussed in the text. The estimates that have been made may all be challenged; some are obviously more open to question than others. However, the gist of the message is clear: the problem of surplus straw production is growing more serious, but it is possible to find ways of utilising greater quantities of this surplus.

FURTHER READING

F.A.O. (1976) *New Feed Resources*. Rome.
Grossbeard (Editor). *Straw Decay and its Effect on Disposal and Utilization*.
John Wiley & Sons Ltd.
MAFF (1950). *Mushroom Growing*. Bulletin No. 34, HMSO, London.
(1970). *Strawberries*. Bulletin no. 95, HMSO, London.
(1977). *Balers and Bale Handling*. Mechanisation Leaflet No. 16.
HMSO, London.
(1981)*Alkali Treatment of Straw*. Leaflet GFG 52 HMSO, London.
(1974), (1976), (1977), (1978) and (1980). *Reports of Straw Utilisation Conferences at Oxford*. (Ed. A.R. Staniforth). ADAS, Oxford.
Staniforth, A.R. (1980). *Cereal Straw*. Oxford University Press.
White D.J. (1975) 'Agricultural and Energy'. *Agricultural Progress*, pp 39-52.

APPENDICES

The National Farmers Union Straw and Stubble Burning Code 1982, and some Examples of Regulations that Apply in Certain European Countries

Uncontrolled straw burning is bad husbandry. It can do serious damage to the environment and bring the agricultural industry into disrepute. Adherence to the code will protect the countryside and help to safeguard wildlife.

Summary

Make an effective firebreak at least 15 metres wide
Never burn when wind conditions are unsuitable
Ensure that burning is responsibly supervised
Burn only during daylight
Inform your neighbours; notify the local fire brigade if required by a local bye-law
Take extra precautions where there is a risk of causing damage or annoyance to the public
Avoid burning on a Bank Holiday and during weekends whenever possible.

Code of Practice

1. Make an effective firebreak consisting of a strip cleared of straw and either thoroughly cultivated or partly ploughed
Remove straw from a strip at least 15 metres wide—straw must be baled or otherwise moved well away from the edge of the firebreak adjoining:
- trees, hedgerows and other wildlife habitats
- roads and public installations
- standing crops

   Remove straw from a strip at least 25 metres wide adjoining:
- dwellings and other buildings—particularly those roofed with thatch, felt or other combustible materials.

   And either cultivate 15 metres of the strip or plough at least the outermost 5 metres.

   It is advisable to burn no more than 12-16 hectares (30-40 acres) at a time; larger fields should be divided up.

Avoid accumulating straw at the edge of the firebreak.

Either cultivate a strip at least 15 metres wide or plough at least 5 metres around any feature listed above.

This table summarises the firebreaks required in various circumstances:

	HAZARD	
	Trees, hedges, other wildlife habitats, roads, public utility installations, standing crops	*Dwellings and other buildings (You should also use the figures in this column when extra precautions are needed, e.g. when a large area is to be burned).*
For Straw		
When burning against the wind . . .		
1. Clear *and*	15 metres	25 metres
2. Cultivate	15 metres	15 metres
or plough	5 metres	5 metres
When burning with the wind . . .		
Create the firebreak as above and clear a further:	30 metres (total 45 metres)	30 metres (total 55 metres)
For Stubble		
Cultivate	15 metres	15 metres
or plough	5 metres	5 metres

REMEMBER—It is an offence under the Highways Act 1980 to start a fire within 50 feet (15 metres) of the centre of a road so as to inconvenience passers-by or damage the highway.

2. Never burn when wind conditions are unsuitable

Consult your local weather service and do not commence burning when:

—the wind exceeds force 3 (8-12 mph); a wind of force 4 moves small branches.

—the direction of the wind is likely to create a hazard from smoke or smuts; especially near:

- buildings, airfields and sensitive horticultural crops.
- roads, particularly motorways and busy holiday routes.

REMEMBER —It is an offence under the **Clean Air Act 1956** to cause a nuisance to the inhabitants of the neighbourhood through the creation of smoke.
—It is an offence under the **Health and Safety at Work etc. Act 1974** to endanger the public while burning straw, for which the maximum fine is **£1,000**.

3. Burn against the wind whenever possible
Where it is necessary to burn with the wind first remove or burn at least 30 metres of straw in addition to the firebreak at the down-wind end of the area to be burned (see table).

4. Avoid burning during prolonged hot and dry weather
Should it be necessary to burn after more than two weeks of hot weather without rain, extra precautions must be taken to avoid damage and the dispersal of smuts over a wide area (for example, burn early in the morning when there is a dew and make wider firebreaks than normal).

5. Ensure that burning is responsibly supervised
At least two persons should be present at all times. One ought to be experienced in straw burning and made responsible for the operation.
Never leave until the fire is completely extinguished. Return later to make doubly sure.
Keep young children well away.

6. Burn only during daylight
Always start as early in the day as possible. Fires which continue burning after sunset cause unnecessary alarm.

7. Always inform:
- your neighbours
- the County Fire Control if required by any byelaw in your area. Give the grid reference of the field if you know it.
- public owners of adjoining land (e.g. Station or Area Manager's Office for railways).
- the local environmental health department if burning near a built-up area.

8. General safety and care
Keep a mobile water-filled slurry tank or crop sprayer with hose attachment on hand for emergencies. Have a stock of fire beaters available.
Know where help can be obtained.
Check that your insurance is adequate and up-to-date. Heavy claims have been made against farmers responsible for straw burning accidents.

BYELAWS
Most district councils in affected areas now have byelaws to control straw burning; check with them to avoid committing an offence.

It is NFU policy that the maximum fine for breach of straw-burning byelaws should be £1,000

N.B. To achieve the most effective burn, spread the straw before burning; keep grain trailer tracks to a minimum.

CHECKLIST

Before you burn, use the following list to check that you are ready to go:

1. Advise your neighbours of your intention well in advance   ☐
2. Check your insurance.   ☐
3. Check the weather forecast for your area.   ☐
4. Notify the fire brigade if required.   ☐
5. Warn your neighbours again prior to burning.   ☐
6. Ensure that a water tanker and fire beaters are available.   ☐

Uncontrolled straw burning is bad husbandry. It can do serious damage to the environment and bring the agricultural industry into disrepute. Adherence to the code will protect the countryside and help to safeguard wildlife.

Additional types of regulations apply in some European countries

i. In *Denmark* local authorities can temporarily ban burning.
ii. Also in Denmark, burning may not take place within 100 m of wooden or thatched buildings or other plantations or stacks or stores likely to catch fire.
iii. In *France* burning is permitted only between sunrise and 4.00 pm under most prefectorial orders. Farmers are required to put out fires before sunset.
iv. In France also fires may not be lit less than 100 m from roads, lanes and paths or 200 m from forests or woods.
v. In order to protect game, stubble should be burnt in 100 m strips or in low winds in France and each year the hunting department Federation set a date before which burning is prohibited.
vi. By prefectorial order a prohibition can be extended to a whole department if there is danger from burning in a particular area.
vii. In *West Germany*, at least in some departments, straw and stubble burning is only permitted outside built-up areas and only between 9.00 am and 7.00 pm Monday to Friday and 9.00 am to 2.00 pm on Saturdays.
viii. In Germany large fields must be divided into 5 m wide strips to a maximum of 3 ha in some departments.
ix. Also in Germany straw may only be burnt against the wind but may not be burnt at all if the wind is strong.

x. Regulations in some German departments require that the remnants of burning be worked into the soil at once.

xi. Another regulation in force in some parts of Germany: if it is the intention to burn an area of 2 ha or more, a local authority must be informed at least two days before the intended burning.

APPENDIX II

REPAYMENTS OF CAPITAL AND INTEREST AMORTISATION TABLE

Annual charge to write off £1,000

Write-off Period (Years)	Rate of interest												
	8%	10%	11%	12%	13%	14%	15%	16%	17%	18%	19%	20%	25%
5	251	264	271	278	284	291	299	305	313	320	327	334	373
6	216	230	237	243	250	257	265	271	279	286	293	301	339
7	192	206	212	219	226	233	240	248	255	262	270	278	316
8	174	188	194	202	208	216	223	230	238	245	253	261	301
10	149	163	170	177	184	192	200	207	215	223	231	239	280
12	133	147	154	162	169	177	185	192	201	209	217	226	269
15	117	132	139	147	155	163	171	179	188	196	205	214	260
20	102	117	126	134	142	151	160	168	178	187	196	205	253
25	94	110	119	128	136	146	155	164	173	183	193	202	252
30	89	106	113	124	133	143	153	161	172	181	191	202	251
40	84	102	111	121	131	141	150	160	170	180	190	200	250

Example: £3,000 is borrowed to erect a building. The annual charge to service interest and capital repayment on the £3,000, repayable over 10 years at 12%, is 3 X £177 = £531. Where the write-off period of the building (10 years) is equal to the repayment period of the loan, then the average annual depreciation and interest will also equal £531.

APPENDIX III

METRICATION

The author apologises to readers who may be frustrated by the use of the metric measures—and assures them that he suffers in the same way. However, much of the information that comes out today is in metric terms and, in the long run, less confusion may arise through using them. The following conversion factors cover the terms that have been used in the preceding pages.

Conversion Factors

1 kilometre (km)	–	0.6214 mile
1 metre (m)	–	1.09361 yard
1 centimetre (cm)	–	0.3937 inch
1 hectare (ha)	–	2.47105 acres
1 tonne (t)	–	0.984207 ton
1 kilogram (kg)	–	2.20462 lb
1 gram (g)	–	0.035274 ounce
1 litre (l)	–	0.219969 gallon
1 megajoule (MJ)	–	947.813 British thermal units (Btu)
1 kilowatt (kW)	–	1.34102 horse power (hp)
1 kilowatt hour (kWh)	–	3.6 megajoules (MJ)

INDEX